bon appetit!

Robert S Swiatek

The Joy of Life Cookbook

The Joy of Life Cookbook

Robert S. Swiatek

formerly ***The Read My Lips Cookbook***

Swiatek Press

First Edition

If you use material found in this book without permission from the author or publisher, we will put you in a pizza oven and cook you. We won't burn down your village, but we will shut down your food supply. Information of a general nature requires no action. When in doubt, contact the author. Mentioning him and the book is greatly appreciated.

Published by Swiatek Press, Inc.
71 Georgian Lane #3
Buffalo, NY 14221

ISBN: 0-9817843-6-4
Printed in the United States

to James, Julia, my mom, and all
the others who inspired my cooking

also by Robert S. Swiatek

The Read My Lips Cookbook:
A Culinary Journey Of Memorable Meals

Don't Bet On It – a novel

Tick Tock, Don't Stop:
A Manual For Workaholics

for seeing eye dogs only

This Page Intentionally Left Blank
– Just Like The Paychecks Of The Workers

I Don't Want To Be A Pirate – Writer, maybe

wake up – it's time for your sleeping pill

Take Back The Earth – The Dumb,
Greedy Incompetents Have Trashed It

Press 1 For Pig Latin

This War Won't Cost Much –
I'm Already Against The Next One

here's your free gift – send $10 for shipping

Mirror, Mirror, On My Car

Table of contents

	Preface to the new edition	i
	Introduction	v
1.	Leaving home: beginning to cook	1
2.	The Triple Cities: a souper time	21
3.	Westchester: where the bread is	47
4.	New England: parties and dinner parties	75
5.	Upstate New York: grow it and keep it	97
6.	The Gulf Coast: brunch time	119
7.	Back to Westchester: camping and tailgating	143
8.	Home again: just desserts	163
9.	Any leftovers?	183
	recipe index	225

Preface to the new edition

The Read My Lips Cookbook was the first book I had published, but not the first one I wrote. That book has yet to be published – maybe, next year. The second one didn't come into print either, although you can find bits and pieces of it in ***for seeing eye dogs only*** and ***wake up – it's time for your sleeping pill***. There's a good chance that my second manuscript will never be published.

Amazingly, my cookbook received lavish praise, including three (out of three) five star reviews from the critics. Others raved about it as well. These fine critics were family, friends and people I have yet to meet, and some whom I met only once. Many of these fine reviews can be found at Amazon.com as well as on the page I have for the book on my web site.

Going back to my earlier years, I recall parts of meals that others fed me. Each Sunday, our family went to the house of Grandma Stella and Grandpa Thomas Choinski – my mom's parents – and I only recall my Grandma's chicken soup. I loved it because she made it with bay leaves, which my mom wasn't fond of. I recently purchased four ounces of the wonderful spice. That should satisfy the needs of about ten families for twenty years – it's an awful lot of bay leaves. Of course, I cherished my mom's cooking, since she inspired so many of the recipes in this book.

Our family traveled to the homes of her four siblings, which included three sisters, my three aunts Adele, Esther and Florence. My Aunt Esther also doubled as my Godmother and I fondly recall numerous visits to her and my uncle Ray's house for dinner. Just walking into their abode overwhelmed me with the aroma of pork chops, mashed potatoes and sweet cabbage on so many occasions. This was food at its best.

During the major holidays of Christmas and Easter, our family might go to these same grandparents' home or to that of my uncles and aunts for a fine meal. Sometime in late afternoon, my mom or dad would round us up – they didn't use a lariat – and say that we had another stop to make at the family of my father's relatives. I was disappointed, but got over that rather quickly when we stopped in to my cousin Dorothy and her husband Ray's home for more food. There's no reason why you can't have two dinners in one day. On those occasions, I recall the delicious potato salad as well as the smoked Polish sausage, not to mention the scrumptious desserts. I should mention that Dorothy – she's not from Kansas – is the butter lamb lady in Buffalo. She and her family are the main reason why Western New York has butter in the shape of the Easter lamb each spring.

Another dinner that my uncle Matthew and aunt Dorothy (a different one) hosted – maybe we were only cousins – featured city chicken and a vegetable Jell-O mold. I liked the food so much that you can find both items in this book.

I was a boy scout for a few years and thought about one merit badge, which I never earned: cooking. You might say that this culinary thing hit me when I was very young. The only food

I recall cooking then was a baked potato on a fire outdoors. We just threw the potatoes into flames and after a half hour or so, we had blackened potatoes – but they were good. Blackened grouper came much later. I recall one camping trip in the late winter or early spring when our scout troop did the cabin thing and fortunately none of us caught the fever. We probably only stayed for one night, but I vividly recall one meal of Campbell's chicken noodle soup and smoked Polish sausage – yummy.

I also recall summer picnics at Crystal Beach – now only a fond memory – and recall the boiled hot dogs, which we couldn't get enough of. Today, I have one or two grilled each year, but back then, I used my parents' gas stove to create hot dogs done the same way, right on the burner flames. I never burned the house down and they never complained. Cooking adventures of mine are featured in each of the nine chapters here, so you'll have to go to those pages.

Thomas Fortenberry is one of the critics who loved my cookbook. I hope to meet him in the near future. He has also reviewed a few other books of mine and truly enjoys all of them – so far. However, he had two criticisms about ***The Read My Lips Cookbook***. He thought it should have been longer – translation: he didn't want it to end since he couldn't get enough of the anecdotes. He also felt that the title didn't quite fit the character of the book. In fact, he thought that the subtitle was more appropriate.

It's been on my mind to republish the cookbook. I had an idea for the cover, which a few collaborators helped out with, but for some time I couldn't come up with a new title. One Sunday morning in the summer of 2009, while in Hammondsport for the Arts and Crafts Festival, I was inspired. It happened at Mass that day. I pondered what the book is really all about. Sure, it's a cookbook, but it's about the love and our fondness for cooking and enjoying the fruits of our labors – pun intended. It's about getting together and sharing a meal and all the happiness and pleasure to be found in that experience. A very unique part of this book is the laughter and joy invoked by way of what's between the recipes, something that can't be found in many cookbooks.

The title that would be perfect to reflect those feelings was ***The Joy of Cooking***. Of course, that was also the name of another endeavor of a few years ago by Irma S. Rombauer and Marion Rombauer Becker. I have it on my bookshelf and it's a great book, in which I have found so many wonderful recipes. I recommend it very highly, and there's no reason why I couldn't use the title. However, in keeping with the thrust of my book, I decided on the title that you see on the front cover. May all your meals be memorable!

Introduction

When children leave their parental home to go out into the world, they are faced with quite a few decisions regarding their new life. A choice they don't have is about eating. Just like you and me, they must eat to live! There are quite a few people who live to eat, but that will not concern us here. In feeding oneself, you have one of three choices:

1. You can go to restaurants (anything from fast food to fine dining.)

2. You can have someone cook a meal for you (a relative or friend.)

3. You can cook something for yourself.

Restaurants are a great pleasure, but only if the food is good. Eating fast food on occasion is fine; I have done it more than once in the past. Fine restaurants still don't guarantee healthy dining all the time. Also, if you eat out a lot, you will eventually get tired of it. Unless you live in a large city like Chicago, New York or Los Angeles, the variety of eating establishments will be limited. You will quickly find that your bankroll is limited as well. This is even more so when times are tough, such as the recessions that we experience from time to time.

Another consideration about restaurants is that the food is not always as good as we expected. Oh, the food may have been good, but we may have hoped it would be better, considering the money we spent. Think of all the occasions when you were slightly disappointed with your meal. I won't even mention those times when the service was lousy.

If we let someone else do the cooking all the time, it's a good way to lose friends. It may be a fine approach to eliminate some unwanted family members, but not recommended. By the way, a spouse falls within the category of friends and relatives. If your spouse is not that good a cook, it's even more imperative for you to be one. If that person lacks culinary skills, it would behoove you to do some cooking and be good at it. It will only strengthen the relationship. Your mate may then be reluctant to say goodbye to you and your good cooking! There must be some truth to the statement, "the way to a person's heart is through the stomach."

It looks as though the third choice is inevitable. You won't stop going out to restaurants if you can afford it. Besides, it's good to get out of the house. In addition, you can go over to have some of mom's cooking every so often and you shouldn't pass up an opportunity to share a meal at the home of a friend or relative. It's just that learning to cook is a requisite.

If cooking seems like such drudgery, how can we make it more palatable? That pun was intended. Four things will do that, namely the food should taste very good, the cost should be small, the food should be good for you and the preparation should be minimal. I don't think anyone will disagree on these points. Two other minor points are to be made. First, you are not embarking on a diet. Second, food that is good for you doesn't necessarily imply so called "health foods." Regarding this last statement, someone wrote a letter a while ago to a food magazine asking for cookie recipes that were made without egg yolks, sugar, salt, butter and margarine. Didn't she want flour omitted too? Anyway, she can eat those cookies; I certainly won't.

What will it take to be a good cook? First of all, you have to accept the fact that you will not become one overnight. It will take time to develop those skills. So start small and work at it. There will be failures, so you have to be willing to adapt. If something doesn't work out to your satisfaction, there are two things you can do about it; you can figure out what went wrong and make appropriate changes so that the next time the result will be a masterpiece. The other option is not to try the recipe again. Who needs the aggravation?

Another quality necessary is being able to follow directions. A recipe will tell you to do things in a certain way. There is a reason for it. Someday you will find that there is a better way and that is fine. Adaptability and good judgment are necessary but they will come with time. When you first start out you will follow instructions to the letter. With experience, you will be able to add certain spices and ingredients to make the dish better. You will also be able to leave out and substitute one component of a recipe for another. But it will take time and experience.

You had better acquire a good sense of humor if you don't already have one. People will make comments about your food that you may not appreciate at times. Just laugh it off and remember that taste is subjective. Over the years, you will find that you will be getting more praises than insults. Remember that you're only human. How does that saying go? "It is better to have cooked and lost than never to have cooked at all."

You will need organizational skills too. This simply means good planning. If you are having a dinner party with two dishes that each require a crock pot, you better either have two crock pots or be able to get a second one on short notice. Little details are more important than you think. If you are cooking a roast of pork in the oven and need the oven for baking chicken wings, you will have to resolve the conflict. The solution may be as simple as using the same oven temperature for both with the roast going on the bottom rack and the wings on the top rack. It may not be that simple, though.

I have been cooking for well over forty years. Some of the highs and lows are chronicled in this book. I have also taught high school math for eight years. This certainly doesn't give me the right to be a cooking teacher, but I do feel very strongly about writing a book on cooking. I have never taken a cooking course but I don't really think it's necessary. I know plenty of people who are excellent cooks and have taken no culinary courses whatsoever.

In a sense, my cooking course took place over the last forty years or so. It was truly a field experience. I myself have been my strongest critic, but there have been others too. I have had the best teachers as well, from my mom and grandmother to many friends in different areas of the country. I have to give credit to Gourmet magazine, whose many recipes I have tried and enjoyed, as well as to the late James Beard. I still have his basic cookbook, the first one I ever bought. It is showing its wear but I cannot recommend it highly enough for the novice as well as the experienced cook. There are many more teachers too numerous to mention.

What makes this cookbook different from all the rest? Certainly you can find books that emphasize the four aforementioned requirements: easy to fix, good, economical and great taste (less filling is not required.) You can also find many cookbooks with plenty of good hints for success in the kitchen. Didn't someone on The Mary Moore Show mention that a good performance in the kitchen would result in being rewarded in the . . . never mind.

This book has all that. It also has humorous anecdotes that should make you smile. It is based on my trips away from my place of birth. It features suggestions for meals as well as parties. It has my experience in it. It starts out slowly but proceeds to achieve the ultimate growth possible. It is not the ultimate cookbook, but one that you will enjoy as part of your collection. Most important, it will be useful and it will be a good teaching tool. Who could ask for anything more? *Bon appétit!*

~~~ Utensils and Tools ~~~

If you are going to do any serious cooking, you will need tools. Here are some of the things that I use as well as others that I don't.

large iron skillet – one of the best ways to satisfy your daily requirement of iron is to cook in an iron skillet

small saucepan – used to cook vegetables and gravies

medium saucepan – used to warm up leftovers and also for vegetables

Dutch oven – for the main course

small skillet – great for a sautéing and can be used for re-heating

covers – you may have a cover for every pot and pan but one cover may be used for more than one pan

blender – I can't see a kitchen without one; you can grind coffee beans, make milkshakes, crush ice cubes, and so on

spatula – one of the greatest kitchen inventions ever

wooden spoons – great for stirring; the old ones hold up the best, while the newer ones seem to be of softer wood

electric mixer – for whipping creams, egg whites, and other uses

mortar and pestle – the only way to grind spices

hand grater – good for grating ginger, carrots, and potatoes

corkscrew – not really necessary if you buy wine drunk out of a bag

toaster oven – throw away your toaster as this oven can take its place and do a lot more

tableware and cutlery setting for eight – you will need it for those dinner parties; use paper and plastic for larger parties

potato masher – I mash potatoes and rutabagas with it, while some prefer to use an electric mixer.

oven thermometer – many ovens are inaccurate; it gives you a better idea of the real temperature

meat thermometer – helps for roasts of pork, beef, or lamb

ovenproof casserole – for dishes that you cook in the oven

bread pans – if you plan to bake bread, you will need two; you can use a cookie sheet to make round loaves

cookie sheets – for oven baking and roasting

metal rack – needed for roasts and to cook chicken wings in the oven

bread bowl – if you are serious about bread baking, this is a must; I received mine as a gift; it is an eight-quart earthenware dough bowl for oven and microwave and I have used it as a punch bowl and for pasta

other implements – steak knives, rolling pin, paring knife, bread knife, carving knife, knife for chopping and mincing, soup ladle, serving spoons and forks, gravy bowl, serving bowl, basting brush, measuring cup and spoons, can opener, plastic containers for storing leftovers, pot holders, dish towels, vegetable steamer, wine glasses, beer mugs, peppermill, wok, metal skewers, charcoal grill, pancake flipper, coffeepot, colander, chopping block, strainer, ice bucket, waffle iron, ice cream maker

You will not need all these tools at once. Buy them as you need them, or ask for them as gifts. The following are some kitchen products that I don't own and probably won't ever buy.

flour sifter – at one time I had one but you really don't have to sift flour

electric flour sifter – people actually buy these things

microwave oven – a vastly overrated kitchen tool; you can warm a leftover item in a small pot on the stove, even if it is frozen solid

food processor – no one actually uses these as they take so much effort to clean and really aren't that good; anyone who has one has it packed away in its original box

dough hook – I am content to make bread with my own hands

ice crusher – you can use your blender to crush ice

capaccino machine – I don't own anything I can't spell

deep fryer – if I want deep fried foods I go to a greasy spoon

meat slicer – I thought about buying one many years ago, but a good carving knife will do just fine

fondue set – the cheese industry would go out of business if they depended on me

egg poachers – anyone who steals eggs should get high cholesterol

battery powered butter warmer – I use solar power for warming my butter

Common abbreviations will be used throughout this book. **Teaspoon** will be abbreviated by **tsp, tablespoon** by **tbsp** and **pound** by **lb.** The number of people that a recipe will serve will be an approximation since some people eat like birds and others like vultures. You will note that the recipes are indexed alphabetically as well as by the type of dish, such as pork dishes, appetizers, desserts and so on. Good luck!

~~~~~~~~~~~
~~~~~~~~~~~

1. Leaving home: beginning to cook

In the summer of 1968, I left home to venture into the world. My destination was the state of New Jersey. I had found a job, teaching math at Mahwah Jr-Sr High School. Being a teacher meant a minimal salary and very few meals at restaurants. I knew I would have to do most of my own cooking, or else mooch meals from fellow teachers – not exactly my style.

When I think back to those days, I recall that I had a few set meals to get me through. I could cook steak for the first day and a friend's mother had given me her recipe for spaghetti sauce, so that would take care of the second day. The family name of Giordano meant a guaranteed recipe of success for a true Italian effort, even if I was Polish. For the third day, I could cook a chicken or turkey potpie or TV dinner as the center of the meal and my own chili recipe would suffice for the next day. On the fifth day, I could try chicken, probably with the help of "Shake and Bake" and for the sixth day would have beef stew from a can over egg noodles. Day seven might be something as simple as hot dogs and the leftovers would carry me over for three more days, at least. You will note that my selections did not include that very familiar dinner of macaroni and cheese.

The first cookbook that I ever owned was the June 1968 printing of *The James Beard Cookbook* in paperback, a book that I cannot recommend highly enough for any serious cook. It is probably the cookbook in my collection that is most worn out and certainly the most used of the lot. Getting back to those early days of cooking for me, this is the way my meals *occurred*. The recipes that follow are the way I would cook them around the time ***The Read My Lips Cookbook*** was published.

~~~ day one ~~~

The best way to cook steak is outside on a grill. The wintertime may put a damper on this idea but there is an alternative: pan-frying. This means cooking the meat on a hot skillet without the use of butter, oil or fat. No matter how you cook the steak, try to minimize the use of salt. The meat has so much flavor by itself that it's not necessary. As for the type of meat, sirloin and London broil are fine. I find that chuck steak, although it costs less, has too much fat and gristle. Another key point is to keep the flavor in by searing the meat. Charcoal briquettes are fine for cooking or even plain charcoal, if you can find it. Just make sure that the fire is hot so that the flavor is locked inside.

grilled steak *serves 6*

2 lbs sirloin steak fresh ground pepper

Rub each side of the steak with ground pepper and place on the grill. Cook for 5 minutes and then turn over. Allow 5 minutes for the second side also, but you can check for doneness by slicing into the steak. How long you let the steak cook depends on how you like your meat: rare, medium, or well done.

pan-fried steak *serves 6*

2 lbs sirloin steak
non-stick cooking spray
fresh ground pepper

Heat an iron skillet over high heat until it is almost smoking. Trim all the fat from the steak. Sprinkle each side with pepper. Spray some non-stick cooking spray on the pan. Place the steak in the pan and let it sear for 1 minute. Turn the steak over and repeat for 1 minute. Lower the heat to medium and cook for 5 minutes and then turn the meat over and cook the other side for 5 minutes. Check for doneness with a knife and serve.

The note about removing the fat before pan-frying reminds me of the time I came home and on opening the door thought the place was on fire. I was overwhelmed by smoke. As it turned out, my friend Spike was pan-frying a steak and he had left some fat on the meat. That's what will happen if you don't remove all the fat from the steak. Timing your meals with a smoke alarm isn't a good idea.

baked potatoes *serves 4*

4 baking potatoes
fresh ground pepper
butter or margarine

Heat oven to 400°. Wrap each potato in aluminum foil and place in oven. Cook for 1 hour and 10 minutes, or until the potatoes are tender. Serve with butter and pepper.

French-style beans *serves 4*

10 oz pkg. frozen French-style green beans
2 tbsp butter 2 tbsp Dijon mustard
¼ cup sliced almonds 1 tbsp lemon juice
If you have a vegetable steamer, steam the beans for 5 minutes. If not, cook the beans according to the package directions. Melt the butter in a small saucepan and sauté the almonds until they are golden brown. Add the mustard and lemon juice, blending well. Add the sauce to the beans and serve.

You can make a salad with spinach, escarole, romaine, leaf or iceberg lettuce and just about any vegetable you desire. Personally, I don't buy tomatoes in the wintertime since they taste like cardboard.

tossed salad *serves 4*

8 leaves of romaine lettuce, shredded
½ cucumber, sliced 3 chopped scallions
1 fresh tomato, cut up salad dressing
½ green pepper, sliced croutons
Mix all the vegetables in a large bowl. If a particular vegetable is not available (such as green pepper or cucumber), it can be omitted. Serve the salad in individual salad bowls; add dressing to each, along with some croutons.

croutons

6 slices of bread   6 cloves of garlic, minced
3 tbsp olive oil

Cut the bread into ½-inch cubes and let dry overnight. In an iron skillet, combine the oil and garlic and sauté over medium heat for 2 minutes or until golden brown. Add bread cubes and stir frequently with a wooden spoon until they are browned.

You can also make croutons by baking them.

baked croutons

6 slices of bread, cubed   garlic powder

Spread bread cubes on a cookie sheet and sprinkle with plenty of garlic powder. Bake at 250° until they are golden brown, checking now and then to be sure they don't burn.

oil and vinegar dressing

1 pkg. Good Seasons dressing   red wine vinegar
dry red or white wine   olive oil

Follow the instructions on the package but instead of using water, use wine.

Credit for this idea goes to Marguerite, who taught with me in New Jersey and knew a few things about good food.

menu for day one

grilled steak	baked potatoes
tossed salad	French-style beans

~~~ day two ~~~

I had the pleasure of sharing an apartment in Buffalo with my friend Spike from the fall of 1969 to early 1970. Spike advocated cooking spaghetti sauce for days on a very low simmer, to blend all the flavors. We made a batch of sauce with ground beef and pork neck bones once and it came out splendid. However, even though the sauce was done, Spike insisted on turning on the heat, to keep it simmering. I would turn off the heat. This went on for a while. Somehow, Spike won out and the sauce kept simmering. Unfortunately, the meat in the sauce disintegrated and the bones turned out as soft as the meat had been. As a result, we had to dump it.

spaghetti with meat sauce *serves 8*

1 tbsp olive oil
2 lbs pork neck bones
6 cloves garlic, minced
1 large onion, minced
2-six oz cans tomato paste
1 cup water
2-28 oz cans tomato puree
1 tsp dried oregano
1 stalk celery, minced
1 cup dry red wine
½ tsp fresh ground pepper
1 carrot, grated
1/8 tsp cinnamon
1 tbsp dried thyme
1 tbsp dried basil
1 tsp salt
1 clove
2 bay leaves
pinch of sugar
1 tbsp dried parsley
1 lb Italian sausage
1 lb meatballs

Heat the oil in a large Dutch oven and add the pork neck bones. Brown on all sides; add minced garlic and onion and cook for 2 minutes. Add tomato paste and water and cook for 5 minutes. Add remaining ingredients, except for the sausage and meatballs, and bring the mixture to a boil. Turn heat down to low and simmer for 5 hours. Remove the pork bones, strip remaining meat from bones and add back to the sauce. Add sausage and simmer for 30 minutes. Make the meatballs, add to the sauce, and simmer for 1 more hour. Remove sauce from stove and place in the refrigerator to cool. Reheat the next day and serve over spaghetti cooked as directed on the box.

meatballs

1 lb ground round steak	½ cup bread crumbs
1 tsp dried basil	1 egg, beaten
fresh ground pepper	1 tbsp olive oil

In a large bowl, mix the first 5 ingredients and form the mixture into approximately 12 meatballs. Heat oil in an iron skillet over medium heat and brown the meatballs on all sides. They are now ready to drop into the sauce.

menu for day two

spaghetti with meat sauce	fresh Italian bread
tossed salad	dry red wine

~~~ day three ~~~

A potpie or TV dinner is not that exciting but it can be a meal if you add a tossed salad, a baked potato, and a vegetable. Since the oven was on anyway for the pie or dinner, why not bake a potato at the same time? Just start the potato ahead of the main entree or else your potato will be slightly crunchy.

cooked beets *serves 4*

6 medium beets
water

Wash beets and cut off the tops, leaving 1 inch or so. Place beets in a small saucepan with enough water to cover them and bring to a boil. Lower the heat and cook until tender, about 45 minutes. Remove beets from the pan and let cool for 5 minutes. Remove outer skin from the beets, slice and serve.

menu for day three

chicken pot pie
baked potatoes
tossed salad
cooked beets

~~~ day four ~~~

By now, you probably think that my friend Spike was a terrible cook, but not so. He was a diligent cooking student and he knew what it was all about. I remember some of the extraordinary beers and stouts that he brewed. He could also make an excellent chili. He once visited me in New Jersey and insisted on making a batch of the stuff. He didn't have all the ingredients that he needed but did a great job of improvising. He started it while I was at work and it would have been superb except for one thing – he fell asleep while it cooked. The burner was set too high and the chili burned on the bottom of the pot. Unfortunately, the burnt taste took over the entire flavor of the dish.

chili con carne *serves 8*

2 lbs ground beef
2 cloves garlic, minced
1 tbsp olive oil
2 large onions, chopped
1 green pepper, chopped
1 stalk celery, chopped
2-28 oz cans tomatoes
1-6 oz can tomato paste
pinch of sugar
fresh ground pepper
¼ tsp cayenne pepper
4 tbsp chili powder
1 tbsp paprika
1 tsp ground turmeric
1 tsp dried oregano
1 tbsp ground cumin
¼ tsp ground cloves
1 tsp ground coriander
¼ tsp ground allspice
¼ tsp ground cinnamon
1 can kidney beans

Brown beef and garlic in olive oil over moderate heat. Add onions, green pepper and celery and cook for 2 minutes, stirring. Add remaining ingredients, except for the kidney beans, and bring to a boil. Lower heat and simmer for 45 minutes. Rinse and drain the kidney beans, add to the sauce, and simmer 5 minutes more. Serve over boiled rice or cooked thin spaghetti, if desired, or simply in bowls with fresh bread.

Note: Ground turkey may be substituted for the beef. To make a vegetarian chili, omit the meat. Any spice that is not available may be omitted. Hot sauce can be substituted for the cayenne; however, the last four spices add a distinctive touch.

menu for day four

chili con carne
tossed salad
fresh bread
beer

~~~ day five ~~~

There are hundreds of recipes for chicken, but baking is one of the easiest and the results are quite good. Chicken is so naturally flavorful that you can bake it without salt or any other seasoning. You can buy chicken parts to your liking or cut up a whole one. The secret to cutting up a chicken is to do the cutting at the joints; don't try cutting the bones, unless they are very thin. You'll get the hang of it after a few tries, but it is well worth the effort since a whole chicken is less expensive than parts. Round out the meal with salad, vegetables, and rice pilaf.

baked chicken *serves 4*

1 fryer, cut up or 12 chicken pieces

Pre-heat the oven to 375°. Soak chicken in cold water for 10 minutes; remove and pat dry with paper towels. Place the chicken on a rack on top of a cookie sheet or large baking pan. Place in oven and bake for 50 minutes. The chicken should be golden brown. Remove chicken from the oven and serve.

rice pilaf *serves 4*

1 small onion, minced
1 tbsp olive oil
1 cup uncooked rice
1½ cups chicken broth
½ tsp dried oregano
½ tsp turmeric
¼ tsp dried tarragon
1 bay leaf

In an iron skillet, sauté the onion in the oil over moderate heat for 2 minutes. Add rice and continue cooking for 3 minutes to coat it, stirring frequently. Add remaining ingredients and bring to a boil. Reduce heat and simmer until broth is absorbed, about 20 minutes. Remove from heat and serve.

steamed vegetables *serves 4*

5 carrots, peeled and sliced
½ rutabaga, peeled and cut julienne style
2 stalks broccoli, cut up
1 tbsp butter
1 tsp lemon juice
1 tbsp brown mustard

Steam the carrots and rutabaga in a vegetable steamer for 10 minutes over low heat. Add the broccoli and steam for 10 more minutes. In a small saucepan, melt butter and blend in the lemon juice and mustard. Pour the sauce over the cooked vegetables and serve.

menu for day five

baked chicken
tossed salad
white wine
steamed vegetables
rice pilaf

~~~ day six ~~~

I am not sure how I picked canned beef stew for a meal, but it tasted all right over boiled noodles. Eventually, I learned how to make egg noodles and surprisingly enough, it's simple. Before long, I discovered that making beef stew was also easy. Not only that, it tasted better, was cheaper and healthier. What you can do is buy a lean bottom round roast and cut it into cubes yourself. If you have a meat grinder or food processor, you can grind some of the roast for hamburger and freeze for another occasion.

beef stew *serves 4*

3 tbsp flour
3 lbs lean beef cubes
1 tbsp olive oil
2 cloves garlic, minced
2 large onions, chopped
1 tbsp dried parsley
1 bay leaf
fresh ground pepper
1½ cups chicken broth
½ cup dry red wine
½ tsp summer savory

Put the flour into a paper or plastic bag and add the beef cubes. Make sure that the beef is covered with the flour. Doing this results in delicious gravy with no effort on your part. In a large Dutch oven, sauté the beef cubes in the oil over moderate heat for 5 minutes or until brown on all sides; add garlic and onions and cook for 3 more minutes, stirring frequently. Add remaining ingredients and bring to a boil. Reduce heat to low and simmer for 1½ hours. Remove from heat and serve over rice or egg noodles.

egg noodles *serves 4*

2 eggs, beaten
flour
pinch of salt

Beat the eggs; add the salt and enough flour to make a stiff dough. The amount of flour will vary depending on the size of eggs. Knead the dough, adding more flour as necessary. Roll out dough with a rolling pin on a board or large surface, adding additional flour to keep it from sticking to the board. Let the dough dry for 1 hour. Cut the dough into 1½-inch wide strips and stack one on top of the other. Cut the strips into noodles about ¼-inch wide. Bring a large pot of water to boil and add the noodles. Bring back to a boil. Lower the heat and simmer the noodles for 15 minutes. Drain and serve.

wilted endive *serves 4*

1 head endive or escarole
2 tbsp red wine vinegar
4 slices of bacon
fresh ground pepper

Wash endive thoroughly and drain on paper towels. Break each piece of endive in half. In an iron skillet, sauté bacon until crisp. Set aside bacon and move the skillet off the warm burner to cool for 2 minutes. Add vinegar and pepper and put the skillet back on the warm burner. Bring vinegar to a boil and add endive. Lower heat and cook until endive is wilted, stirring occasionally. This should take about 7 minutes. Remove endive to a serving dish, crumble bacon on top and serve.

dilled carrots *serves 4*

6 medium carrots
water
1 tbsp butter
fresh dill or dried dill weed

Peel carrots and cut into ¼-inch slices. Place in a small saucepan, cover with water and bring to a boil. Lower heat and cook for 10 minutes or until carrots are tender. Remove carrots to a small serving dish; add butter and dill, and serve.

menu for day six

beef stew
wilted endive
dry red wine
egg noodles
dilled carrots

~~~ day seven ~~~

A hot dog for dinner, with a salad and French fries, is not that unusual and only somewhat good for you. I was at my parents' house for lunch one Saturday and we had hot dogs on fresh mini-sub rolls. The wieners were above average and the rolls and sauerkraut made them more delectable. I can't recall too many occasions on which I've had a more enjoyable frankfurter.

When I was growing up, my mother would make us baloney and onions on numerous Saturday afternoons. I also remember a time during my first year away from home when I ordered a baloney and onion sandwich on Italian bread at some small place in South Orange, New Jersey. From those two encounters, I created my own version of the same dish.

baloney and onions *serves 2*

2 tbsp olive oil	4 frankfurters
2 large onions, chopped	fresh ground pepper
1 green pepper, chopped	Italian or rye bread

Heat the oil in heavy iron skillet over medium heat and add, onions and green pepper. Cook until the onions and pepper are almost transparent, about 5 minutes. Cut up the franks into ½-inch pieces and add to the pan along with the ground pepper. Cook for another 5 minutes. Remove from the pan and serve with fresh rye or Italian bread.

potato salad *serves 6*

6 large potatoes
water
1 cucumber, peeled and chopped
1 small onion, minced
1 tbsp paprika
fresh ground pepper
1 cup mayonnaise
3 tbsp prepared mustard
½ green pepper, chopped

Wash potatoes thoroughly and cut each in quarters. Place in a medium-size saucepan, cover with water and bring to a boil. Lower heat and cook for 15 minutes or until potatoes are soft. You can test for doneness with a toothpick or fork. Drain potatoes and let them cool. When they have cooled down, cut them into ½-inch cubes and put them into a large bowl. Add the remaining ingredients and blend. Add more mayo if the salad is too dry. Serve.

menu for day seven

baloney and onions
rye bread
tossed salad
dill pickles
potato salad

Customer to waitress: Give me a rubber band sandwich and make it snappy!

~~~~~~~~~~~~~~~~~~~~~~
~~~~~~~~~~~~~~~~~~~~~~

2. The Triple Cities: a souper time

I didn't stay long in New Jersey – only a year – and then I moved to the city of Buffalo to share an apartment with my friend Spike. He soon left to get married. Not long after that, I moved to Binghamton, New York, in the fall of 1970. I was set to study computer science at the university while teaching high school math part-time. As you can imagine, my salary was less than in Mahwah and I was to have less free time.

Binghamton is one of the Triple Cities and also home of the "speedie". A speedie is perfectly legal and has nothing to do with drugs. It's a combination of marinated pork and lamb in various proportions. Personally, I prefer the pork without the lamb. The meat is placed on metal skewers and then broiled over a charcoal fire – or gas grill, if you're so inclined. It is then served on a slice of Italian bread. Various restaurants in that area sell it and you can purchase the marinated meat at butcher shops and grocery stores in most cities. Speedies are currently made out of chicken as well. Either type is delectable and worth trying.

By that time I had some practice in cooking and started collecting a few recipes. The secret to any good recipe, in my opinion, has to do with three basic premises:

1) Does it taste good to you?
2) Is it easy for you to make?
3) Is the cost to make it reasonable?

A recipe won't work if there is an ingredient in it that you don't like. If you don't care for liver, no recipe with liver in it will satisfy the first premise. I don't cook dishes that I won't eat. If you prepare a dish for dinner guests that you refuse to eat and they don't like, who is going to eat it? You may ask how to tell if a recipe in a cookbook will be good. Well, look at the ingredients. Then try it yourself. It will give you a very good idea.

The second consideration has to do with effort. After trying a recipe you will know how much work it takes on your part. If quite a bit of effort is involved, but the result is extraordinary, you may still want to keep the recipe. It's your decision. Don't confuse effort with the length of time a dish takes from start to finish. For example, sauerbraten takes from four days to a week to get ready, but the effort needed is minimal. Baking your own bread could take an elapsed time of three hours. If you see a recipe that goes on for columns and columns in a book, chances are it won't be worth the effort.

The last consideration is cost. Some ingredients are outrageous in cost. For example, saffron costs more than some illegal drugs. However, it is a wonderful spice and you won't need that much of it – a little goes a long way. There are other ingredients that are expensive and you may not be able to get by with just a small amount. You will have to decide on the cost issue. You may be able to substitute an ingredient and save money. The results may be even better than the original recipe.

This brings me to another point. You have to be able to use your judgment, common sense, and past experience when cooking. Not too long ago I tried a recipe for pistachio soup. I like pistachios, the soup could be served hot or cold, and it looked like a good recipe. I made it and the consensus was that it was *all right*. I agreed but since I had spent a great deal of time with preparation (mostly in shelling those little nuts), I decided to forego the recipe in the future.

On another occasion I tried a recipe for soup with celery and walnuts, among other ingredients. My guests didn't vomit over it, but the general consensus was that it was too crunchy. I should have chopped the celery thinner and ground the walnuts rather than chopping them. Another solution may have been to use a blender, even though the recipe just said to chop the ingredients. In any case, the effort was small, so I might try the recipe again.

I had a minor disaster when I tried a recipe for bouillabaisse. The ingredients listed cost a fortune to begin with and I made the mistake of reheating the soup. The mussels in the dish consequently spoiled and I had to toss it before someone started tossing up. First of all, use less expensive fish. As long as it is fresh it won't matter. Second, never cook mussels in a stew or soup – warm only.

Around the same time, I tried to make salmon bisque. The only error I made was to use canned salmon. It was a very big mistake. It was edible, but that's about all. My brother Ken said it tasted chalky but it probably could have been used to clean the toilet. You get the idea. The lesson I learned was that I should have used fresh salmon. Nevertheless, soups and stews are easy to make and almost a meal in themselves. Add a salad and some bread and *voilá*!

~~~~~~~~~~~
~~~~~~~~~~~

~~~ day eight ~~~

When you make fish chowder, any kind of fish will do, such as cod, haddock, scrod, pollock, pout or a mix. Just be sure that it's fresh. The chowder will taste better the next day as it seasons. It can be frozen as well.

fish chowder *serves 8*

4 slices of bacon
1 large onion, minced
1 green pepper, minced
3 tbsp flour
1 tsp dried basil
½ tsp fennel seed, crushed
28 oz can tomatoes
2 large potatoes, cubed
fresh ground pepper
2 tbsp butter
2 lbs fresh haddock

In a large Dutch oven, fry the bacon until it is crisp. Remove bacon and set aside. Add the onion and green pepper to the pan and cook over medium heat for three minutes. Add flour and continue cooking for three minutes more, stirring frequently. Add the basil, fennel, tomatoes, potatoes and ground pepper and bring to a boil. Lower heat and simmer until the potatoes are tender, about thirty minutes. Crumble the bacon. Add butter, bacon and haddock and cook for five minutes more. Turn off the heat and let the chowder stand for ten minutes. Serve.

Making beans requires one step before the actual cooking. The beans have to soak for a few hours. This can be done overnight or you can bring the beans to a quick boil, cook for two minutes and let them stand for one hour. One way is as good as the other.

hickory baked beans *serves 8*

1 pound pinto beans
2 cups water
6 slices bacon, cut up
1 can tomato soup
3 tbsp brown mustard
¼ cup molasses
½ cup brown sugar
½ cup ketchup
1 tsp liquid smoke

Soak the beans overnight or use the quick method as described above. Place soaked beans into a large Dutch oven and add water. Bring to a boil, lower the heat and cook for one hour. Add remaining ingredients and bring back to a boil. Lower the heat and simmer for one hour. Serve.

menu for day eight

fish chowder
tossed salad
dry white wine
hickory baked beans
Russian brown bread

~~~ day nine ~~~

Some people consider gazpacho a cold soup while others consider it a liquid salad. It's actually both. I had my first taste of it in a New York City restaurant. I liked it so much that I decided to try to make it myself. The best part about this recipe is that it's so easy. Just let the blender do all the work.

gazpacho *serves 6*

4 large tomatoes	1 tsp ground cumin
1 cucumber	¼ cup olive oil
1 green pepper	¼ cup red wine vinegar
1 large onion	1 tsp Creole seasoning
3 garlic cloves	1 tsp chili powder
1 cup tomato juice	garnishes as desired

Slit tomatoes with sharp knife and submerge them into pan of boiling water for 1 minute. Remove, cool slightly, peel them and cut into quarters. They should peel easily. If not, put back into water for another minute. Peel cucumber (if it's fresh, there is no need to peel) and cut into quarters. Remove insides of green pepper and quarter. Peel onion and garlic and quarter them. Put half of vegetables into blender with half the tomato juice. Puree for thirty seconds and pour into large pitcher. Repeat with remainder of vegetables. Add remaining ingredients and stir. Refrigerate overnight. Ladle into bowls and add any or all of the following as garnishes: chopped cucumber, chopped green pepper, chopped onion and croutons.

beer and beef stew *serves 4*

2 lbs lean beef cubes	3 large onions, chopped
3 tbsp flour	12 oz of beer
fresh ground pepper	1 tsp summer savory
2 tbsp olive oil	1 tsp dried thyme leaves
1 tsp salt	

Dredge the beef in the flour and the pepper. Heat the oil over moderate heat in a large Dutch oven and add the beef cubes. Brown on all sides; add the salt and onions and cook for three minutes. Add the beer, summer savory and thyme. Bring to a boil. Lower heat and simmer for one hour. Serve over steamed rice or egg noodles.

menu for day nine

gazpacho	beer and beef stew
tossed salad	egg noodles
beer	

~~~ day ten ~~~

You can make your own coating for chicken by combining bread crumbs with an assortment of spices, rather than buying the more popular store brand. This coating can also be used on fish and pork chops.

This reminds me of the time that I lived in Buffalo and we had a party at our apartment. Spike no longer lived with me but another teacher had moved in to help pay the rent. Since I had to work nights, I was going to be late for the party so I had to delegate cooking the chicken to Harry, my housemate. I prepared some chicken coating mix and Harry had to do the rest. The chicken turned out good but a few days after the party I noticed a funny smell in the kitchen. The garbage had been removed so it wasn't that, but I could not figure out what it was. A day or so later the smell was worse. I finally figured out what the rotten smell was: before Harry cut up the poultry, he removed the internal organs and instead of throwing them in the garbage, he put them in the kitchen pantry. Whew!

tasty baked chicken *serves 4*

1 chicken, cut up | coating mix

Wash the chicken and shake pieces dry. Place some of the coating mix in a plastic or paper bag and add the chicken pieces, a few at a time. Shake the bag to coat thoroughly. Repeat with the remaining pieces. Place chicken pieces on a rack on top of a cookie sheet and bake for fifty minutes in a 375° oven. Remove from oven and serve.

To make bread crumbs, dry a few pieces of bread overnight. Place the bread slices into a blender, a few at a time and turn on the blender until you have bread crumbs. It couldn't be easier. Now you have a use for stale bread.

chicken coating mix *for about 3 chickens*

2 tbsp dried minced onion	2 tbsp paprika
1 tsp celery seed	1 tbsp chili powder
4 cups bread crumbs	½ tsp dried mustard
½ cup olive oil	fresh ground pepper

Crush the minced onion and celery seed in a mortar and pestle. Put the bread crumbs into a large bowl and stir in the oil, mixing thoroughly. Add the crushed onion, celery seed, and the remaining ingredients and blend well. The coating can be stored in the refrigerator.

Bacon is easier to cut if it is frozen or only slightly thawed. I store it in the freezer, since it keeps longer that way. When I need a slice or two, I cut perpendicular to the way the slices run. Thus, I cut an amount of small pieces equivalent to the number of slices that I need. This also eliminates the need to crumble the bacon later.

bean with bacon soup *serves 8*

1 ½ cups pea beans	3 large onions, chopped
4 slices bacon	½ tsp sugar
¼ tsp dried sage	2 quarts of water
½ tsp dried thyme	1 tsp Tabasco sauce
1 tbsp olive oil	fresh ground pepper
2 garlic cloves, minced	3 tbsp vinegar

Soak the beans overnight or use the quick method (*see the hickory baked beans recipe*). Sauté the bacon in a heavy iron skillet until crisp. Remove the bacon, drain on a paper towel; discard the drippings. Crush the sage and thyme in a mortar and pestle. Add oil to frying pan and sauté the garlic, onions, sugar, sage and thyme until the onions are brown. Be careful not to burn them, but the darker they are, the better the flavor will be. The sugar helps to brown them. Place beans into a large Dutch oven and add the browned onions and water. Bring to a boil, lower the heat and simmer for 1½ hours. Turn off the heat, crumble the bacon and add it, along with the Tabasco sauce, ground pepper and vinegar. Stir well. Serve with croutons made from dark bread, using the crouton recipe but substituting dark bread.

menu for day ten

bean with bacon soup
tasty baked chicken
baked potatoes
Italian bread
tossed salad

~~~ day eleven ~~~

I've always wanted an easy recipe for minestrone soup, but it seems all the recipes are so complicated. Here is a recipe that you'll find enjoyable and easy to make. You can use any combination of beans that you have around, such as pinto, green or yellow split peas, lentils, black, pink, Great Northern, navy, or baby lima. Just don't use jelly beans.

turkey minestrone soup *serves 8*

2 tbsp green split peas
2 tbsp yellow split peas
2 tbsp lentils
2 tbsp navy beans
2 tbsp pinto beans
2 tbsp black beans
2 tbsp Great Northern beans
2 tbsp pearl barley
2 cloves garlic, minced
1 large onion, chopped
2 stalks celery, chopped
1 turkey drumstick
1 cup dry red wine
4 carrots, sliced
½ tsp dried thyme
pinch of sugar
28-oz can tomatoes
½ tsp dried oregano
1 tsp dried basil
fresh ground pepper
1 cup water

Soak beans overnight. Drain and place into a soup pot along with all the other ingredients. Bring to a boil, lower the heat and simmer until the turkey is tender, about 2 hours. Remove turkey and let it cool. Separate the meat from the bone, gristle and tendons. Chop the turkey meat and add back to the minestrone. Serve with any kind of crusty bread.

One of the dishes that I recall from childhood was hamburgers with onions and tomatoes. It sounds like a simple dish, which it is, and it's also delicious and quite easy to make.

stewed hamburgers *serves 6*

3 lbs lean ground beef
1 egg, beaten
1 cup bread crumbs
1 tsp dried basil
1 tbsp olive oil
3 large onions, sliced
1 28-oz can tomatoes
pinch of sugar

In a large bowl, mix the ground beef with egg, bread crumbs and basil. Heat oil in a heavy iron skillet over moderate heat. Form hamburger mixture into patties and brown on both sides. Remove to a Dutch oven. Repeat until all the hamburgers are browned. Add the remaining ingredients and bring to a boil. Lower the heat and simmer for one hour. Serve the hamburgers on hard rolls dipped in the sauce and covered with the onions.

menu for day eleven

turkey minestrone soup
corn on the cob
hard rolls
stewed hamburgers
tossed salad

~~~ day twelve ~~~

You can't beat an Easter ham from the Broadway Market in Buffalo. The only other one that comes close is a Virginia baked ham. You may wonder what to do with a ham, other than baking it and making ham sandwiches. Actually, numerous dishes use ham in one way or another. I will include a few throughout this book. One soup you can make with ham or a leftover ham bone is yellow split pea. It's easy and delicious.

yellow split pea soup *serves 8*

2 cups yellow split peas	½ cup chopped rutabaga
1 smoked ham hock	2 quarts of water
1 carrot, finely chopped	fresh ground pepper
1 small onion, chopped	2 slices of ham, chopped

Place the split peas into a large pot with the ham hock (or ham bone,) carrot, onion, rutabaga, and water. Bring to a boil, lower the heat and simmer for 2 hours. Remove the ham hock and let it cool. If there is any meat on it, cut it up and add to the soup. Add the ground pepper and ham and simmer for another ½ hour. Serve.

The next recipe calls for soy sauce and mayo. You can use any brand you like, but my preference is Kikkoman Lite soy sauce and Hellmann's mayonnaise. Kikkoman seems to have a more distinctive flavor. It costs a little bit more than the others, but I think it's worth it. As far as mayonnaise goes, Hellmann's makes a Light and a cholesterol-free variety in addition to the regular.

tuna macaroni salad *serves 8*

1 lb elbow macaroni
6 oz can tuna in water
1 cucumber, chopped
1 small onion, chopped
fresh ground pepper
2 tbsp soy sauce
½ cup mayonnaise

Cook macaroni according to the package directions. Drain and cool. Drain the tuna. Place the macaroni into a large bowl; add tuna and the remaining ingredients. Mix and, if necessary, add more mayo. Refrigerate. Serve with basil tomatoes.

basil tomatoes *serves 4*

4 large tomatoes, sliced
1 tbsp dried basil
2 tbsp olive oil

Place the tomatoes in a glass dish. Sprinkle with basil and olive oil. Toss gently and marinate for two hours in a cool place. Do not put in the refrigerator, as the tomatoes will lose their flavor. Serve.

When I first began to cook, I used powdered ginger. Now I always use gingerroot, which I grate myself. If you use the root instead of the powder, you will need a hand grater. The one I use I've had for years and it has served me well. I also suggest keeping gingerroot in the freezer. It lasts longer and more important, it's easier to grate when frozen.

Chinese cauliflower *serves 6*

1 head cauliflower	¼ cup orange juice
1 tbsp butter	2 tbsp soy sauce
1 green pepper, thinly sliced	½ cup water
1 tbsp grated gingerroot	1 tbsp cornstarch

Trim the cauliflower and place into a medium saucepan, cover with water and bring to a boil. Lower the heat and simmer for ten minutes. Remove from the stove and drain. In a small saucepan over medium heat, melt the butter. Add green pepper and ginger and sauté for 3 minutes. Add orange juice and soy sauce and cook for 1 more minute. In a small bowl, mix the water and cornstarch, dissolving the cornstarch. Add to the green pepper mixture, stirring. Raise the heat and cook until sauce thickens. Place the cauliflower on a serving plate, pour the sauce over it and serve.

menu for day twelve

yellow split pea soup
basil tomatoes
French bread
tuna macaroni salad
Chinese cauliflower

~~~ day thirteen ~~~

In Binghamton, I lived on the second floor, above my landlord. You may have seen those little bottles of root beer extract on shelves in the grocery store. I doubt that you could find them today, but at the time, I bought one and in the spring of 1971, I started to make my own root beer in a gallon jug. All you have to add is water, sugar and yeast to the extract and let it brew for a few weeks. This I did according to the package directions, but I noticed that not much seemed to be happening. I added some more yeast.

A day or two later, I went out to play softball. When I returned, the back door to my place was wide open and the floor was much cleaner than when I had departed. My root beer had exploded and the liquid somehow dripped downstairs into the landlord's apartment. He probably heard the explosion too. I had to do some explaining as well as cleaning up. I noticed some tiny fragments of glass, not much larger than grains of sand. It must have been some explosion. My landlord probably thought the house was being attacked.

The lesson from that episode is simple: follow directions. You can improvise for certain situations but not for others. The root beer directions also said to keep the jug on its side and capped with a cork, if possible. Had I done that, the cork would have shot out and there would have been some liquid on the floor, but certainly no explosion.

chicken shadow soup *serves 8*

3 quarts of water
1 bay leaf
¼ tsp dried sage
¼ tsp dried thyme
4 carrots, sliced
2 stalks of celery, sliced
2 large onions, chopped
1 package chicken soup mix
fresh ground pepper

Put the water, bay leaf, sage, thyme, carrots, celery, and onions into a large soup pot and bring to a boil. Lower the heat and simmer until vegetables are soft, about fifteen minutes. Add the soup mix and simmer for ten minutes more. Season with ground pepper and serve with egg noodles.

Dried beans are reasonably cheap and loaded with protein and numerous vitamins. They are also said to be a fine way to lower your cholesterol. You can make the next recipe with great northern, pinto, pink or black beans. Smoked sausage adds a zestful flavor.

Cajun beans and rice *serves 4*

1 ½ cups pinto beans
2 cups water
1 bay leaf
1 green pepper, chopped
1 large onion, chopped
¼ tsp cayenne pepper
1 celery stalk, minced
2 tbsp paprika
8 oz tomato sauce
2 cloves garlic, minced
½ tsp Tabasco sauce
1 tbsp chili powder
¼ lb smoked sausage, sliced

Soak the beans overnight. Drain. Place in a large Dutch oven, add the water and bay leaf and bring to a boil. Lower the heat and simmer for 1 hour. Add remaining ingredients, except for the sausage, and simmer until the beans are tender, about 1 hour. You may need to add more water as the beans cook. Add the sausage and simmer for fifteen minutes more. Serve over boiled rice.

Boiled rice can be made quickly and is loaded with carbohydrates. Just remember to use twice the amount of water as of rice.

boiled rice *serves 6*

2 cups long grain rice
4 cups water

Place the rice and water in a medium saucepan; bring to a boil. Lower the heat and simmer for twenty minutes or until all the water is absorbed. You can stir occasionally. Serve.

menu for day thirteen

chicken shadow soup
Cajun beans
steamed rice
egg noodles
tossed salad

~~~ day fourteen ~~~

During my third year in the Triple Cities of Endicott, Binghamton and Johnson City, I shared an apartment with two college students. I cooked some of the time but John and Tom did some of their own cooking. I mentioned that I was never a big macaroni and cheese dinner aficionado. One day, John made himself some, but it turned out watery. Apparently, he hadn't drained the macaroni before adding the cheese sauce. He didn't follow directions on the box.

On another occasion, I made beef stew for everyone and John cooked some lima beans – not one of my favorites but healthy nonetheless. A day or two later, John warmed up the stew together with the lima beans. I didn't have any.

At that time, a store on the outskirts of town sold horsemeat. Thom and Linda, good friends of mine who lived in nearby Pennsylvania, would fix it for me but not tell me that sometimes the meat could be found at the racetrack. I enjoyed whatever they fixed and couldn't tell the difference between cow and horsemeat, even though I felt it could have been the latter.

One day, I made some hamburgers from horsemeat. I believe the recipe was the one for stewed hamburgers in this chapter. John liked it and finished it up, since I couldn't eat it. Somehow, all I could think of was Mr. Ed.

A quick meal for any occasion is fish. You can cook certain types of fish on the grill outside, such as salmon, swordfish, halibut, tuna, monkfish and mahi-mahi. Baking and poaching is easy, too, and quick. Any kind of fish will do, as long as it is fresh. Today, even fish in the supermarket is quite fresh. You can use haddock, cod, pollock or scrod for the following recipe.

baked fish *serves 4*

nonstick vegetable spray	¼ tsp garlic powder
2 lbs haddock	½ tsp dill weed
1 tbsp lemon juice	¼ cup rye bread crumbs

Spray a baking pan with the nonstick spray. Place the fish into the pan and sprinkle with lemon juice, garlic powder and dill weed. Cover with bread crumbs and bake at 375° for 15 minutes. Serve with rice pilaf and a dry white wine.

During my teens, my mother used to fix a soup made from cabbage and potatoes. It seemed like a simple soup but was very flavorful. My version of the soup is a little different, but still tasty.

potato sprout soup *serves 4*

1½ lb brussels sprouts
2 cups chicken broth
3 large potatoes
½ lb smoked Polish sausage
fresh ground pepper

Clean the brussels sprouts and trim. Place sprouts in a medium saucepan and cover with broth. Bring to a boil, lower the heat and cook for 10 minutes. Remove brussels sprouts from the broth. In a blender, coarsely chop sprouts. Cut potatoes into ½-inch cubes and put into saucepan with the broth. Bring to a boil, lower heat and cook for ten minutes. Add brussels sprouts and sausage and simmer for ten more minutes or until the potatoes are tender. Season with ground pepper and serve.

chicken broth *makes 2 quarts*

2 cups of water
½ tsp salt
1 bay leaf
2 tbsp parsley
1 celery stalk
chicken necks, wing tips and backs

Put all ingredients into a soup pot and bring to a boil. Lower heat and simmer for two hours. Remove chicken wing tips and celery stalk and discard. Remove chicken backs and necks, separate any meat from the bone, and save for another use.

menu for day fourteen

potato sprout soup
rice pilaf
dry white wine
baked fish
tossed salad

The following conversation took place at a restaurant following dinner between my sister Pat and her daughter Elizabeth, who was then three years young:

Pat: *That was very good. Elizabeth, are you full?*
Elizabeth: *No, I'm empty.*

~~~~~~~~~~~~~~~~~~~~~~
~~~~~~~~~~~~~~~~~~~~~~

3. Westchester: where the bread is

I left the Triple Cities to head across the Hudson River. My new home was to be Wappingers Falls, noted for nothing much until an event a few years ago, which I won't get into. It had nothing to do with cooking. Within a short time, I found myself moving into my first house in the grand old county of Westchester.

Appropriately enough, it was here that I really started to make bread. I don't think that you'll have to think about that one too much. But seriously, this was where I developed my ability for the art of making bread. I don't precisely recall in which town I tried my first recipe for bread. I do remember that it was Cuban bread from ***The James Beard Cookbook*** and it was a big flop. The result would have made an excellent paperweight or boat anchor, so I threw it out.

The good thing about this disaster was that I didn't completely give up. It may have taken some time, but nonetheless at some point I tried to bake bread once again. The result was much better and eventually each new attempt proved to be an improvement over the last one. Not only did I like the bread, but my guests commented on how good it was. I knew I had done something right. I really believe that anyone can make bread. It is not that difficult. It takes a few hours from start to finish, but your effort is minimal, from fifteen to twenty minutes in all. The secret for baking bread includes three key points:

1. patience
2. the yeast mixture
3. the kneading process.

As far as patience goes, most yeast dough breads need to rise twice for approximately one hour each. The actual baking will take close to another hour, so the whole process will take about three hours. I made some onion bread recently. I mixed the dough together, put it into a warm oven, and went out for an hour walk. When I returned, the dough was ready for its second rise. You don't have to take a walk between risings, but you can do something else, such as leaving the house. That way, the three-hour time frame will not even matter. The aroma wafting through your home while the bread is baking will also inspire you to do it again. This brings up the idea of patience on another plane. If your first attempt does not turn out exactly as you would like, don't give up. Try again and again. Your perseverance will pay off.

The second important point is the yeast mixture. This applies to yeast breads as well as to quick breads, as you will see in the next paragraph. I will concentrate on yeast breads for now. Any bread that you try will be a failure without yeast. Burning the yeast has the same effect as no yeast and your effort will be worthless. It is critical NEVER TO BURN THE YEAST. You can avoid burning by using almost lukewarm water or liquid to proof the yeast. *Proofing* means dissolving in water or milk with a pinch of sugar. Also, remember to cool down any mixture into which you add the yeast mixture. An ice cube or two should do the trick.

For quick breads, the process is similar but easier. You need to have an active catalyst, baking powder in most cases. If the baking powder is old, the bread may not rise. See to it that the ingredient has not expired. If no rising takes place, the result will be a rock rather than bread. That's why my first bread attempt failed.

As far as the type of yeast to use, I used the solid cake yeast in my first few bread attempts. I have not used it since, but rather I use the package yeast, which is easier to find on supermarket shelves. One is as good as the other. Generally speaking, wheat and rye breads will require 2 packages of yeast. You can probably get away with one for bread that uses only white flour.

The last point has to do with kneading the bread. *Kneading* means taking the bread dough into your hands and working it so that the ingredients are blended together. Most recipes call for five to ten minutes of kneading. I usually knead bread for one or two minutes. The reason I use less time is because, by the time I put the dough on the board to knead, the ingredients are well blended. That's because I use a huge mixing bowl. It is made of earthenware, seven inches high and thirteen inches wide at the top. I've had it for over thirty years and it cuts down on kneading time. I use a long wooden spoon for mixing to assist in the process. If you can find a bowl like this one, I'd recommend it for use not only in bread baking but also whenever you are mixing something in a large quantity. It can even double as a punch bowl.

Here are some other points about baking bread. I usually warm the oven to about 90° to let the dough rise. It is not essential, but using the oven means drafts are eliminated and I've been doing it this way for years with great success. Sugar is necessary to interact with the yeast. It is not necessary to proof the yeast with the sugar, but if you get into the habit of doing it this way, you'll never forget the sugar in a recipe. The amount of flour to use brings up a good point: I never measure the flour in any bread recipe. If a recipe calls for wheat, rye and white flour, I add some rye flour, some wheat flour and then the amount of white flour depends on when the dough is the way I like it. It's a matter of judgment. You'll get the idea. When pouring the dough onto the surface for kneading, if you try to scrape the dough from the wooden spoon it will stick to your fingers. Instead use a jerky shoving motion to get the dough off the spoon. As far as determining when bread is finished baking, tap the loaves with your fingers. A hollow sound indicates the bread is done. Above all, have patience in your bread baking endeavors. Good luck!

~~~~~~~~~~~
~~~~~~~~~~~

~~~ day fifteen ~~~

Bread is always best right out of the oven. Even a day or two later it is still better than any bread you can buy. The darker breads tend to keep their flavor longer than the white breads. If you ever have coffee left over from a meal, put it into a plastic container in the freezer. You can use it in this recipe for brown bread.

Russian brown bread *makes 2 loaves*

2 packages dry yeast	2 tbsp caraway seed
1 tbsp sugar	1 tbsp anise seed
½ cup lukewarm water	1 tbsp fennel seed
2 cups leftover coffee	1½ cups rye flour
½ cup molasses	1½ cups wheat flour
3 tbsp vinegar	1 cup wheat bran
¼ cup cocoa	6 cups white flour
2 tbsp olive oil	corn meal

In a small bowl, proof the yeast with the sugar in the water. In a small saucepan over moderate heat, add the leftover coffee (or water), molasses, vinegar, cocoa and olive oil. Stir occasionally and remove when cocoa and molasses are dissolved. Pour mixture into a large mixing bowl and cool to lukewarm. Crush the caraway, anise and fennel seeds in a mortar and pestle and add to the cocoa / molasses mixture. When mixture is cooled down (use an ice cube if necessary), add the yeast mixture. Add in the rye flour, wheat flour and bran; mix, stirring vigorously with a wooden spoon. Add white flour gradually and continue mixing until dough is stiff. Turn the dough onto a floured board and knead for about 2 minutes or until dough is smooth and elastic. Wash out mixing bowl, dry out thoroughly and grease with olive oil. Put dough back into the bowl, cover with a damp towel and put into a warm oven to rise until double in bulk, about 1 hour. Divide the dough in half and form each into a ball. Place each on a cookie sheet sprinkled with corn meal, flatten slightly, cover with the damp towel and put back into the oven. Let it rise for about 40 minutes or until nearly double. Remove the towel and bake in a 375° oven for 55 minutes. Remove and cool on a wire rack. Serve.

If you like Creole and Cajun foods, you'll find this next recipe to your liking. It has a rich blend of flavors. Jambalaya can be made with seafood as well, but I find this recipe with ham, chicken and pork sausage to be delightful. I think you will too.

jambalaya *serves 6*

2 cloves garlic, minced
2 tbsp olive oil
1 green pepper, chopped
1 large onion, chopped
½ lb Virginia ham
2 cups cooked chicken
½ lb pork sausages
1 28-oz can tomatoes
pinch of sugar
1 tsp dried thyme
1 tsp chili powder
2 cups long grain rice
fresh ground pepper
4 cups water

Sauté the garlic in olive oil in a large Dutch oven over moderate heat for 2 minutes. Add green pepper and onion and cook for 2 minutes more. Cut ham and chicken into ½-inch cubes and the pork sausages into ¼-inch slices. Add all remaining ingredients and bring to a boil. Lower the heat and simmer until all liquid is absorbed, about 30 minutes. If rice is not thoroughly cooked, add more water and continue simmering. Remove and serve.

A variation on this recipe – one of my favorites – is jambalaya pasta. Just leave out the rice. Cook the pasta separately and while the base is simmering. Drain the pasta and add to the jambalaya. A better idea is to make the jambalaya without the pasta on the day before, and just cook the pasta on the day of the party.

horseradish broccoli *serves 4*

4 stalks of broccoli	1 tbsp olive oil
2 cups of water	1 tbsp mustard seeds
1 tbsp butter	1 tsp lemon juice
1 tbsp olive oil	1 tbsp horseradish

Trim and cut the broccoli into serving size pieces. Place it into a medium saucepan with water and bring to a boil. Lower the heat and simmer for 6 minutes. Meanwhile, in a small saucepan over moderate heat, melt the butter. Add olive oil and mustard seeds and cook until mustard seeds stop popping, about 2 minutes. Add the lemon juice and horseradish and stir. Drain broccoli, pour sauce over it and serve.

menu for day fifteen

Russian brown bread	jambalaya
tossed salad	horseradish broccoli

~~~ day sixteen ~~~

After my Cuban bread disaster, I eventually tried the recipe again and got it right. I'd go further than that. The recipe is fantastic because it tastes great but also requires little time. The result is a crusty bread that tastes so good that there probably won't be any left over. The only ingredients are water, flour, sugar and yeast. This bread only has to rise once so it's quicker than most bread recipes. Give it a try and you won't be disappointed.

Cuban bread *makes 2 loaves*

1 package dry yeast
2 cups lukewarm water
1 tbsp sugar
7 cups flour
olive oil or cornmeal

Proof the yeast in the water with the sugar in a large mixing bowl. Add flour gradually, stirring vigorously with a wooden spoon. Add enough flour to make a stiff dough. Knead the dough for 1 or 2 minutes. Wash, dry and grease mixing bowl with olive oil and add the dough. Cover with a damp towel and place in a warm oven to rise until double in bulk, about 1 hour. Punch down the dough, cut the dough in half and form 2 long loaves. Place on a greased cookie sheet or one covered with corn meal, slash with a sharp knife in a few places and let rise for 5 minutes. Turn on the oven to 400°; place a pan of boiling water in the oven under the loaves. Bake the loaves for about 40 minutes or until they are brown and crusty. Serve hot out of the oven.

chicken cacciatore *serves 4*

handful of fresh oregano
2 cloves garlic, minced
1 tsp dried basil
2 tbsp olive oil
1 frying chicken, cut up
4 tbsp flour
1 28-oz can tomatoes
fresh ground pepper
2 tbsp chopped parsley
1 large onion, chopped
1 green pepper, chopped
1 tsp sugar
½ cup dry red wine
1 cup sliced green olives

Mince the oregano. Use 1 tsp of dried oregano if fresh is not available. Sauté garlic, oregano and basil in oil in a large Dutch oven over moderate heat for 2 minutes. Dredge chicken parts in flour and brown each piece in the Dutch oven. Add all remaining ingredients, except for the olives and bring to a boil. Lower heat and simmer for 25 minutes. Add olives and simmer for 15 more minutes or until chicken is done. Serve over thin spaghetti or boiled rice.

menu for day sixteen

chicken cacciatore
tossed salad
dry red wine
spaghetti
Cuban bread

~~~ day seventeen ~~~

Quick breads are easy to make and take less time than yeast dough because you only have to let it rise once. Irish soda bread can be made with buttermilk or you can sour ordinary milk by adding vinegar with the same results. The following recipe is especially tasty and needs no butter, as it's in the dough.

Irish soda bread *makes 1 loaf*

2 cups milk
2 tbsp vinegar
½ cup raisins
4 cups flour
½ cup sugar
2 tbsp caraway seed
1 tsp baking soda
2 tsp baking powder
1 tbsp butter, melted
1 tbsp sugar
2 tbsp butter, cut into bits and softened

In a large mixing bowl, combine milk and vinegar. Submerge raisins in hot water. In another bowl, combine flour, ½ cup sugar and 2 tbsp butter and work with your fingers. Squeeze water from raisins; add to the dry mix with the caraway, baking soda and baking powder. Mix thoroughly, add the milk mixture, and stir until all ingredients are blended. Grease a heavy iron skillet with butter and pour the batter into the skillet and even it out with a spatula. Heat oven to 350°. Pour melted butter over the dough followed by the sugar. Bake for 45 minutes or until bread is done. An inserted toothpick should come out clean when done. Remove from oven, turn bread onto a rack and cool completely. Serve.

green split pea soup *serves 8*

2½ cups green split peas
2½ quarts of water
2 tbsp parsley
1 stalk celery, chopped
1 bay leaf
1 smoked ham hock
1 large onion, chopped
fresh ground pepper
¼ lb Polish sausage

Put all the ingredients, except for the Polish sausage, into a large Dutch oven, and bring to a boil. Lower heat and simmer for 2 hours. Remove bay leaf and ham hock and put any meat on the ham hock back into the Dutch oven. Cut the Polish sausage into ¼inch slices and add to the soup. Simmer for 10 minutes more. Serve.

escarole orange salad *serves 6*

1 head of escarole
½ cup chopped pecans
2 oranges
¼ cup lemon juice
½ tbsp sugar
1 tbsp Dijon mustard
¼ cup olive oil
fresh ground pepper

Thoroughly wash escarole and drain. Separate leaves and break each into bite-size pieces. Put escarole into a large salad bowl and add pecans. Peel oranges and cut lengthwise into quarters and then cut each into ¼ inch slices. Add to the escarole. Mix the lemon juice, sugar and mustard until they are thoroughly blended. Add oil in a stream and blend in completely. Add to salad with the ground pepper and toss. Serve.

Rutabagas are almost peasant food insofar as they are plain and cheap. They have a taste that stands by itself and are also easy to prepare.

mashed rutabagas *serves 4*

1 rutabaga	fresh ground pepper
water	1 tbsp butter

Peel, slice and cut the rutabaga into French fry pieces. If you have a French fry cutter, use it. Put rutabaga into a medium saucepan and cover with water. Bring to a boil. Lower heat and simmer until tender, about 10 minutes. Remove the pot and drain. Mash rutabaga, add pepper and butter and serve.

menu for day seventeen

Irish soda bread	green split pea soup
escarole orange salad	mashed rutabagas

~~~ day eighteen ~~~

There is nothing like a good rye bread. An important ingredient in any rye bread is caraway seed. If you don't like caraway seed, do not despair. You can make rye bread without the caraway. Dill adds flavor as well.

dill rye bread *makes 2 loaves*

2 packages dry yeast
2 cups lukewarm water
1 tsp sugar
1½ cups milk
olive oil
2 tbsp caraway seed
1 tbsp dill seed
1 tsp salt
2 cups rye flour
4 cups white flour

Proof yeast in the water with the sugar. Pour the mixture into a large mixing bowl and add milk, 1 tablespoon of olive oil, the caraway, dill and salt. Add rye flour and stir vigorously. Add white flour gradually, stirring to blend in ingredients. Add enough white flour to make a stiff dough. Roll dough onto a floured board and knead for about 2 minutes. Wash and dry the mixing bowl and grease with olive oil. Put dough into the bowl and cover with a damp towel. Put bowl into a warm oven and let dough rise for about 1 hour or until double in bulk. Remove dough, divide in half and form into 2 loaves. Put loaves into 2 greased bread loaf pans, cover with a damp towel and let rise until doubled, about 40 minutes. Remove the towel and bake at 375° until loaves are golden brown, about 45 minutes. Remove from the pans, cool and serve.

While the bread is baking, you can prepare the main course: poached fish. Don't start it too early since the fish will only take about fifteen minutes to cook.

poached cod *serves 4*

3 tbsp flour
2 lbs of cod
1 tbsp olive oil
4 oz tomato sauce
½ cup dry red wine
1 tsp dried dill weed
2 tbsp dried minced onion

Put flour into a plastic bag and add fish, a piece at a time. Shake the bag to coat each piece with flour. Heat oil in a large iron skillet over moderate heat. Add the pieces of cod, skin side up and cook for 1 minute. Turn pieces over and cook the second side for 1 minute. Mix tomato sauce, wine, dill and dried onion and add to skillet. Bring liquid to a boil and lower heat. Simmer for 10 minutes or until cod is done. It will flake when done. Serve with wine sauce over boiled rice.

menu for day eighteen

dill rye bread
poached cod
boiled rice
tossed salad

~~~ day nineteen ~~~

Most seafood can be prepared in an instant. In fact, it will take you no longer to cook fresh fish than to warm a prepared entree from the sea. The only exception to this would be if you use a microwave oven. Even then, the time difference is minimal. Shrimp is especially delectable and quick to cook. Don't overcook it, as it will turn out rubbery. Here is my recipe for scampi. It is loaded with garlic.

shrimp scampi *serves 4*

2 lbs of medium shrimp	3 tbsp olive oil
6 cloves garlic, minced	2 tbsp butter

Peel shrimp and wash thoroughly. Sauté garlic in olive oil and butter in a heavy iron skillet over medium heat for 5 minutes. The garlic should change color but do not burn it. Add shrimp and cook until it turns pink, about 2 minutes. Remove and serve over rice pilaf.

One of the best vegetables for you is the onion. As you can tell, I use it in all types of recipes. You can use onions to make tasty bread. The fragrance of the vegetable from this recipe will overwhelm your home.

onion rye bread *makes 2 loaves*

2 large onions, sliced thin and chopped
olive oil
1 tbsp sugar
2 packages dry yeast
2 cups lukewarm water
3 tbsp caraway seed
1 tbsp dried dill weed
2 cups rye flour
3 cups white flour

In a heavy iron skillet, sauté the onions in 2 tablespoons of olive oil for 10 minutes, over moderate heat. Raise the heat, add 1 teaspoon of sugar and continue cooking onions until they are golden brown. Cool. Meanwhile proof yeast in water with the remaining sugar. Pour mixture into a large mixing bowl and add caraway seed, dill weed and cooked onions. Make sure the onions have cooled down. Add rye flour and stir. Add white flour gradually, stirring vigorously to blend in ingredients. Add enough flour to make a stiff dough. Roll dough onto a floured board and knead for about 2 minutes. Wash and dry the mixing bowl and grease with olive oil. Put dough into bowl and cover with a damp towel. Put bowl into a warm oven and let dough rise until double in bulk, about 1 hour. Remove dough, divide in half and form into 2 loaves. Put loaves into 2 greased bread pans, cover with damp towel and let rise for about 45 minutes or until doubled. Remove towel and bake at 375° until loaves are golden brown, about 45 minutes. Remove from the pans, cool and serve.

menu for day nineteen

shrimp scampi
rice pilaf
dry white wine
onion rye bread
tossed salad

~~~ day twenty ~~~

One meal that stands out in my mind from numerous occasions is a roast of pork. A boneless pork roast is quite expensive, but a cheaper roast such as a loin is also good. I don't cook pork that often, but when I do, it becomes a feast. Pork must be cooked thoroughly, and it takes about thirty minutes per pound to cook at 375°. Use a meat thermometer to determine when the roast is done. Insert the thermometer into the fleshiest part of roast and make sure it doesn't touch the bone. The pork will be done when the thermometer registers 175°.

The good thing about cooking a pork roast is that you can use the oven to cook vegetables such as carrots and potatoes simultaneously. One of the first pork roasts I cooked was when friends visited me in Binghamton. The meal included carrots and potatoes cooked with the roast, as well as salad and wine. I even captured the complete spread on film. It was quite a meal, even while a record snowstorm was burying the city outside.

roast loin of pork *serves 6*

2 tbsp dried rosemary
1 tsp dried thyme
4 lbs loin of pork
1 tsp garlic powder
fresh ground pepper
6 large carrots, peeled
4 large potatoes, washed and quartered
4 medium onions, peeled

Preheat oven to 375°. Crush rosemary and thyme in a mortar and pestle and rub the roast with it, along with garlic powder and ground pepper. Insert a meat thermometer into roast without touching the bone and place in the oven. Cook until thermometer registers 175°, about 2 ½ hours. While the roast is cooking, cut carrots in half and then cut them in half lengthwise. Add potatoes, carrots and onions to the roast during the last hour of cooking. Remove roast and vegetables from the oven and let stand a few minutes before carving. The pork drippings can be used to make gravy, if you desire. Serve the pork and vegetables with applesauce.

Horseradish and applesauce may sound like a strange combination but it is delicious. Over one weekend I fixed it for my friends Thom and Linda, and their sons, Karl and Ben. The latter was not even six years old but he loved the combination and remembers it fondly even today. If you can please a youngster, you must have made something good.

spicy applesauce *serves 4*

6 large apples
¼ cup water
¼ cup sugar
1 tsp ground cinnamon
¼ tsp ground cloves
2 tbsp horseradish

Peel and core apples. Cut into quarters and cut each quarter into ¼-inch pieces or smaller. Put apples into a medium pan with the water, sugar, cinnamon, and cloves and bring to a boil. Lower the heat and simmer for 10 minutes. Put apples into a serving dish and blend in the horseradish. Serve.

The following bread should go nicely with the roast of pork. For that matter it will probably go well with just about anything. The people I made it for were impressed with its taste.

cinnamon raisin bread *makes 2 loaves*

1½ cups milk
4 tbsp margarine
¼ cup sugar
2 packages dry yeast
1 cup lukewarm water
3 tsp cinnamon
½ cup raisins
8 cups white flour
2 eggs
olive oil

In a small saucepan on medium heat put milk, margarine and all but 1 teaspoon of the sugar. Stir occasionally and remove from heat when the sugar is dissolved and margarine melted. Pour into a large mixing bowl and cool. Proof the yeast in water with the remaining sugar. Add cinnamon and raisins to milk mixture and when the mixture is lukewarm, add the yeast mixture. Add 2 cups of flour and stir vigorously. Add eggs and beat them into the dough. Add as much more flour as necessary to make a stiff dough. Roll dough onto a floured board and knead for about 2 minutes. Wash and dry the mixing bowl and grease with olive oil. Put dough into the bowl, cover with a damp towel and place in a warm oven to rise until double in bulk, about 1 hour. Turn dough onto a floured board, cut in half and shape each into a loaf. Put each loaf into a greased bread pan, cover with a damp towel and return to the oven to rise until doubled, about 40 minutes. Bake loaves in a 375° oven for about 45 minutes, or until golden brown. Remove and cool on a wire rack. Serve.

Gravy can be made from the drippings of a pork roast, turkey, chicken or roast of beef. You can use flour or cornstarch to thicken the gravy. If gravy is left over, don't throw it away. Save it to put over egg noodles or plain rice or into soups, casseroles or stews. It is a good addition to any of these.

pork gravy *serves 4*

pork drippings
¾ cup of water
2 tbsp cornstarch
fresh ground pepper

Skim fat from the top of the drippings. If you put drippings into the refrigerator overnight, the fat will rise to the top and solidify and be easy to separate. Put the drippings and ½ cup of water into a small pan. Bring to a boil. Mix cornstarch thoroughly in ¼ cup of water and add to drippings in the pan, while stirring. Bring to a second boil, lower heat and simmer until gravy is thickened. Season with ground pepper. Serve.

The following recipe can be cooked in a wok or in an iron skillet on the stove if you don't have a wok. You can substitute sweet vermouth if you're out of sherry.

Chinese cabbage *serves 4*

1 lb of cabbage
3 tbsp olive oil
2 tbsp soy sauce
½ tbsp cornstarch
2 tbsp brown sugar
¼ cup sherry
4 tbsp vinegar

Cut cabbage into inch squares. Heat oil in the wok over high heat. Add cabbage and cook for 2 minutes. Mix remaining ingredients in a measuring cup and add to the cabbage. Cook for 5 more minutes or until the cabbage is tender. Remove and serve.

menu for day twenty

roast loin of pork with gravy
roasted vegetables
cinnamon raisin bread
spicy applesauce
Chinese cabbage
spicy applesauce

~~~ day twenty-one ~~~

Over the years, I have run across some unusual barbeque sauce recipes. One has pitted prunes in it and another I made myself at a friend's house. The sauce with the prunes is very good and the sauce I made was improvised. It seems that the ingredients were limited so I used what I could find. Even so, the chicken we used this barbeque sauce on came out quite good. Fire must have magical powers for transforming anyone into a good cook.

You can put just about anything you like into your barbeque sauce and it will be good. You will note that I said "just about anything" not anything you want. You still need to use good judgment. The recipe that I have included here is quite simple. One note of caution: just make as much as you will use because the sauce may spoil in the refrigerator since it has no preservatives.

barbequed chicken *serves 4*

1 chicken, cut up
barbeque sauce

Start a fire in the grill using charcoal briquettes. When the coals are ready, place chicken pieces on the grill. Cook chicken on each side for 20 minutes. Apply sauce to each side and cook 10 minutes more per side. Serve.

barbeque sauce *for 1 chicken*

½ cup catsup
3 tbsp brown mustard
1 tbsp liquid smoke
2 tbsp olive oil
¼ tsp cayenne pepper
1 tbsp brown sugar
1 tbsp Worcestershire sauce

Bring all ingredients to a boil in an iron skillet. Lower heat and simmer for ½ hour. Remove and use.

raisin rye bread *makes 2 loaves*

½ cup raisins
1 bottle dark beer
½ cup molasses
olive oil
2 packages dry yeast
½ cup lukewarm water
1 tbsp sugar
3 tbsp caraway seeds
2 cups rye flour
4 cups white flour

Soak the raisins in hot water. In a small saucepan on medium heat put 6 oz of the beer, molasses and 2 tbsp of the olive oil. Stir occasionally and remove after 5 minutes. Pour into a large mixing bowl; add the rest of the beer and cool. Proof yeast in water with sugar. Squeeze out excess moisture from raisins. Add the yeast mixture, caraway seeds and raisins to the liquid. Add rye flour and stir vigorously. Add as much white flour as necessary to make a stiff dough. Roll the dough onto a floured board and knead for about 2 minutes. Wash and dry the mixing bowl and grease with olive oil. Put dough into the bowl, cover with a damp towel and place in a warm oven to rise until double in bulk, about 1 hour. Turn dough onto a floured board and cut the dough in half. Form 2 round loaves and put on a greased cookie sheet. Cover with a damp towel and put into oven and let rise for about 40 minutes or until double in size. Bake in a 375° oven for 45 minutes. Remove to a wire rack and cool. Serve.

menu for day twenty-one

barbequed chicken
potato salad
raisin rye bread
tossed salad

A man was arrested in Washington, D.C. for trying to mail a watermelon using food stamps.
George Carlin

~~~~~~~~~~~~~~~~~~~~~~
~~~~~~~~~~~~~~~~~~~~~~

4. New England: parties and dinner parties

I resided in the Hudson Valley and Westchester area for over seven years. That's why the last chapter was so long. From there, I moved to New England, specifically Derry, New Hampshire. My job was that of a computer consultant, with contracts in nearby Massachusetts. When you think of New England, the first thing that comes to mind is people who talk funny. They say certain words and leave out the letter "r", such as chowda (chowder) and pahk the cahh (park the car.) The reason they do that is because they need that letter for other words that don't have the "r", such as dater (data to us normal folks.)

To say that New England was the first place I had a dinner party would be incorrect. If you consider a dinner party to be any event in which you cook for friends, then my first dinner party was in the first few months after I left home. I have had a dinner party in every place I have lived. As far as parties go, I consider every party that I have thrown to be a dinner party, since each has had plenty of food. The real difference is that one is a sit-down dinner and the other a buffet. Another difference is the number of guests. A party which is not a dinner party is one in which there are plenty of people, drinks, pretzels, potato chips, popcorn and not much else. I've been to those parties and I'm sure you have too.

Clearly, you can see that when I use the term party, I mean dinner party. As it turns out, it won't matter whether there are two or two hundred guests; only the amount of food cooked will vary. The basic rules remain the same and can be summed up as follows:

Try to plan items that can be prepared ahead of time.

Try to plan items that can be frozen.

No more than forty percent of the menu should consist of new recipes.

Since you would like to have time with your guests, any work that you can do ahead of time will be to your advantage. For example, you can make meatballs and certain soups weeks ahead of time and freeze. Just don't forget to thaw the item on time. You can also prepare ingredients beforehand. For example, the cabbage in the Chinese cabbage recipe in the last chapter could be chopped and its corresponding sauce could be prepared ahead of time. This would minimize your time in the kitchen since all you have to do is sauté the cabbage, add the sauce and simmer. Many dishes taste better the next day anyway, so why not make the entree the day before. All that is left is to warm the dish. A salad and its dressing can be made ahead of time, so that all you must do is add the dressing and toss. You get the idea. From a psychological point of view, if you use this approach you won't be inundated with work. There is still plenty to do but you have control of everything.

If you are expecting a good crowd of people (you may not even have the foggiest idea of how many), plan some items that can be frozen in case there are plenty of leftovers. It is only common sense. For one New Year's Eve party in the Triple Cities, I cooked and cooked, expecting a large number of people. As it turned out, less than ten people made the scene. Fortunately, I was living with two college students and I froze some of the items, so leftovers weren't a problem. In addition, the advantage to using this method is peace of mind. Last but not least, do not be afraid to try new recipes on your guests. Just don't try too many new things at one time. My friend Jesse was commenting on my bouillabaisse disaster not long ago. He mentioned that I had so many different items on that occasion that the failure was hardly noticed. There's nothing like a good cover-up. If sixty percent of your items are ones that you have cooked before, you can't go wrong.

If you follow these three bits of advice, you'll have a good party. All you are really doing is planning in advance. That is the secret to eliminating worry and concern.

When I invite a few people for dinner, say six or less, I start with some kind of appetizer and homemade bread and butter. Some of the new butter substitutes are quite good and may be better for you than the real thing, so I use them as well. The appetizer may be some kind of chicken wing recipe, shrimp if I have a little extra money that week, stuffed mushrooms or sausage, which I make from time to time. On occasion, I have had corn chips and store-bought salsa. You can even make your own salsa. There are quite a few good appetizer recipes around which are easy to make.

The next course is soup of some kind, which I probably made the day before. Then comes the main course with salad, some vegetable and rice pilaf, potatoes or noodles. The finishing touch is dessert and coffee. This will be a very nice dinner party for a small number of people.

If you increase the number of people, you have a buffet dinner party. What I do is add an appetizer or two and make another type of bread and another type of soup. If it's relatively warm outside, I may have one cold soup as well as one hot one. I add another main dish or two, plus a few more vegetable dishes, such as baked beans and salads. I really don't make that many desserts, but sometimes people bring them so I am not lacking in that area. As far as running out of food, don't worry about it. If one dish is gone quickly, the others will take up the slack. No one will starve. I have yet to have a party where all the food was consumed. Throughout the next few chapters, I have included some menu ideas for parties. Bottoms up!

~~~~~~~~~~~~~~~~
~~~~~~~~~~~~~~~~

~~~ day twenty-two ~~~

One of the best parties I gave was an impromptu event between Christmas and New Years Eve. I didn't really plan it. I just asked around if people were interested in a party and enough said yes. I quickly planned some food that would be good, but easy. The result was about fifteen people with plenty of good food, drink and music.

Precisely what the full menu was is unclear to me now, but I do remember cooking a roast of beef. Someone even took a picture of me carving the roast. You can do an eye of round, but it is expensive. A simple bottom round is just as good. The most difficult part is carving the beef, but you can even get around that by having someone else do it for you. People feel important if you ask them to carve. Another possibility is to carve some of the roast and leave the knife around for others to do their own hacking. This is not a good idea if you have people from the Bates Motel at your party.

roast round of beef *serves 6*

3 lbs bottom round roast fresh ground pepper

Rub the roast with the ground pepper. Insert a meat thermometer into the roast and place on a wire rack in a baking pan. Heat the oven to 325° and place the pan in the oven. Cook the beef until the roast is done to your liking. Rare will take about 21 minutes per pound, medium rare about 24, medium about 28 and well-done about 33. You can also use the thermometer method: 120° for rare, 130° for medium rare, 140° for medium and 150° for well done. I like beef medium rare, so even if I use a thermometer, I time the meat depending on the weight rather than have the meat reach a certain temperature. You can always cook the roast more if you think it is too pink; if the meat is well done, there's nothing you can do to recover to medium. If you cook the roast medium, the end pieces will be close to well done anyway, so that you can please everyone.

garlic cauliflower *serves 6*

1 head cauliflower
3 cloves garlic, minced
2 tbsp butter
¼ cup bread crumbs

Wash cauliflower, separate into pieces and place into a medium size pan. Add enough water to cover and bring to a boil. Lower the heat and simmer for 10 minutes. In a small pan melt butter and sauté garlic over medium heat for 2 minutes. Stir in the bread crumbs and cook for 1 minute. Drain cauliflower and put into a serving dish, add the crumb mixture and toss lightly. Serve.

menu for day twenty-two

roast round of beef
baked potatoes
garlic cauliflower
tossed salad
dry red wine

~~~ day twenty-three ~~~

A party without chicken in one form or another is no party. Compared to other meats it is quite cheap and there are so many ways to fix it. In addition, it's hard to mess up chicken. I suppose if you cook it too long or not long enough there will be problems. You can buy it on sale, store it in the freezer and you'll be ready for your next party. You don't have to wait for a party to serve this next dish.

Oriental chicken stew *serves 4*

1 chicken, cut up
2 tbsp olive oil
¼ cup soy sauce
¼ cup sherry
1 large onion, chopped
2 stalks of celery, chopped
2 cloves garlic, minced
¼ cup sweet vermouth
¼ cup water
2 tbsp cornstarch
fresh ground pepper

Soak chicken in water for 10 minutes, drain and pat dry. Brown both sides of chicken pieces in the oil in a large Dutch oven on medium heat. Add remaining ingredients, except for water and cornstarch, and bring to a boil. Lower the heat and simmer until chicken is tender, about 40 minutes. Remove chicken to a serving dish and bring sauce to a boil. Mix cornstarch with water and stir into the stock. Cook until sauce is thickened. Return chicken to the pot and warm in the sauce. Serve over boiled rice.

In my opinion, the squash with the best flavor is acorn. Because of its shape, about the only thing you can do with acorn squash is to bake it.

Fortunately, there are various ways to do so and the effort is minimal. Here is one way.

baked acorn squash *serves 2*

1 acorn squash
2 tbsp butter
2 tbsp brown sugar

Cut the squash in half and remove the seeds and pith. Put 1 tablespoon of butter and 1 tablespoon of brown sugar in each cavity and bake in a preheated 400° oven for 1 hour or until the squash is tender. Remove from the oven and serve.

menu day twenty-three

Oriental chicken stew
boiled rice
baked acorn squash
tossed salad

~~~ day twenty-four ~~~

During my stay in New Hampshire, my sister Pat and her husband at the time, Rick, visited from Western New York. We took off for some deep-sea fishing and caught eight fish in all: cod, cusk and haddock. I invited my brother Ken and his wife at the time, Laurie, to join the three of us in a fish feast. They resided nearby just outside Boston. I cooked some of the fish using the recipe for poached cod from chapter 3, except that I used white wine instead of red. Everyone thought the meal was delicious. Fish doesn't come any fresher.

I froze the remainder of the fish and my sister took it back home for my parents. I did keep one small cod for myself in the freezer. I remember it was too small to fillet. About a month later, I cooked it in a little butter in a frying pan. I'll never forget how delicious it tasted; it was almost as good as fresh.

poached haddock *serves 4*

2 tbsp olive oil
3 tbsp flour
2 lbs haddock
2 tbsp Dijon mustard
3 tbsp lemon juice
¼ cup dry white wine

In a heavy iron skillet, heat the oil over moderate heat. Put flour into a paper bag and dredge each piece of haddock in flour. Put haddock into the skillet, skin side up and brown each piece. Turn each piece over and cook for 1 more minute. Mix mustard and lemon juice in a small bowl and add wine. Stir to mix. Pour wine mixture onto haddock and bring to a boil. Lower the heat and simmer until haddock is done, about 5 minutes. Serve.

Besides doing your own cooking, you can also make your own salad dressing. A blender makes this process very easy indeed. The following recipe for Russian dressing can be made with chili sauce, instead of ketchup. When I was younger, just about every summer my mother would make at least one batch of chili sauce. Not too long ago I used some of her sauce in place of the ketchup. You can't compare chili sauce from the supermarket with the kind my mother made. I have also used this dressing as a dip for vegetables at a party or two.

Russian dressing *makes 1 ½ cups*

1 cup mayonnaise ½ cup ketchup
2 tbsp horseradish 1 tsp Worcestershire sauce
Put all the ingredients into a blender and mix until completely blended. Refrigerate.

menu for day twenty-four

poached haddock rice pilaf
French-style beans dry white wine
tossed salad with Russian dressing

~~~ day twenty-five ~~~

Many people eat meat every day of the week. On the other side of the coin, some people never eat it. I remember one party when the husband of one of the women I worked with admitted to being a strict vegetarian. He wouldn't even eat Jell-O. I was thankful that I had prepared quite a few different dishes so that there were at least some he could eat. Fortunately, he is an exceptional case.

I fall somewhere in between these two extremes. There are days when I don't eat meat, but I am certainly not a vegetarian. Meat is a very important part of everyone's diet. You need protein. Besides, if you don't eat meat, how can you enjoy a delicious steak or a mouthwatering roast of pork or a pizza with sausage, peppers and onions?

When I first left home, one of my early meals had Spanish rice as the heart of it. Unfortunately, it was from a can and not homemade. Spanish rice is relatively easy to make, costs pennies and you can make it as hot as you like. I recall seeing a cookbook (though I can't remember which one) that said to use 1/4 teaspoon of cayenne pepper in a recipe, more if you're Spanish. Does that mean that people who are not Spanish can't take the heat or maybe that Spanish people are immune to hot spices?

Spanish rice *serves 6*

3 slices of bacon	2 cups uncooked rice
1 clove garlic, minced	1 tbsp paprika
1 large onion, chopped	8 oz tomato sauce
1 green pepper, chopped	4 cups chicken broth
pinch of cayenne pepper	2 cups uncooked rice
1 tbsp chili powder	pinch of saffron

Sauté bacon with garlic in a heavy iron skillet until bacon is crisp. Add onion and green pepper and continue cooking for 2 more minutes. Add remaining ingredients and bring to a boil. The saffron is optional. Lower the heat and simmer until all liquid is absorbed, about 20 minutes. Serve.

menu for day twenty-five

Spanish rice	dilled carrots
tossed salad	Italian bread

~~~ day twenty-six ~~~

They say the worst kind of food is cafeteria food. There were a few meals in high school that I thought weren't so bad. One in particular was American chop suey or what I call noodles and ground beef. You don't even need beef to make this. You can use ground pork or better yet, ground turkey. The flavor is completely different if you use turkey instead of beef, but delicious nonetheless. The dish is cheap, loaded with carbohydrates and easy to fix. You can use tomato sauce or tomato puree and change the spices to your liking.

Atlantic chop suey *serves 8*

1 tbsp olive oil
2 cloves garlic, minced
1½ lbs ground turkey
1 green pepper, chopped
1 large onion, chopped
28 oz tomato puree
pinch of sugar
½ tsp dried oregano
fresh ground pepper
1 tbsp paprika
1 lb cooked macaroni

In a large Dutch oven heat oil over moderate heat and sauté garlic. Add ground turkey and cook until browned. Add green pepper and onion and cook for 2 minutes. Add tomato puree, sugar, oregano, ground pepper and paprika and bring to a boil. Lower the heat and simmer for 35 minutes. Cook macaroni according to directions on the package and drain. Pour meat sauce over cooked macaroni, stir thoroughly and serve.

sweet and sour red cabbage *serves 6*

4 slices of bacon
1 onion, chopped
2 stalks celery, chopped
¾ cup cider vinegar
¼ cup molasses
2 tbsp brown mustard
8 cups shredded red cabbage

Fry bacon in a heavy iron skillet until crisp. Remove bacon, crumble and set aside. Add onion and celery and cook until tender, about 5 minutes. Stir in vinegar, molasses and mustard and bring to a boil. Add cabbage, stir and cook until tender, about 20 minutes. Stir in bacon and serve.

menu for day twenty-six

Atlantic chop suey
tossed salad
sweet and sour red cabbage
fresh bread

~~~ day twenty-seven ~~~

I remember a meal from the high school cafeteria called mock chicken legs. It wasn't chicken and I wasn't that crazy about it. I'm not sure what went into it. Maybe it's better that I don't know! This is true about much of the food we eat, especially at Chinese restaurants. I really don't want to know what goes into some of those dishes.

One dish that reminds me of mock chicken legs is "city chicken." As you might guess, it's not chicken at all, but a delight nonetheless. It is a mix of pork and veal, skewered on wooden sticks, breaded and simmered. This is my version of the recipe.

city chicken *serves 6*

3 lbs lean pork cubes
1 lb veal stew
wooden skewers
2 eggs
½ cup water
½ cup bread crumbs
fresh ground pepper
2 tbsp olive oil
1 onion, finely minced
½ cup dry white wine

Put pork and veal on skewers in ratio of 3 to 1. It should take about 6 pieces of meat per skewer. Scramble eggs in a small bowl, add water and stir to blend. Dip skewered meat in egg mixture and then roll around in the bread crumbs. Season with ground pepper. Heat oil in a heavy iron skillet and brown meat on all sides. Add onion and wine and simmer until meat is tender, about 1 hour. Serve with rice pilaf.

Jell-O molds are great for parties. You can make them with fruit, vegetables, or a combination of both. You are limited only by your imagination. Besides, they are healthy, easy to make and everyone will love them.

vegetable Jell-O mold *serves 6*

1 package lime Jell-O	8 oz crushed pineapple
¼ head cabbage	2 carrots, grated

Make Jell-O according to package directions and refrigerate. Meanwhile, chop and grate cabbage in a blender. Drain pineapple. When Jell-O is starting to set (about thirty minutes), add the cabbage, pineapple and carrots and stir to blend. Pour mixture into a Jell-O mold or plastic bowl and return to refrigerator. To unmold the Jell-O, dip the mold in lukewarm water and turn the Jell-O onto a serving plate.

menu for day twenty-seven

city chicken	rice pilaf
tossed salad	vegetable Jell-O mold

~~~ day twenty-eight ~~~

Pilafs can be made with regular rice, brown rice or cracked wheat. Brown rice will take about twice as long to cook as regular rice. Bulghur or cracked wheat will take as long to cook as brown rice unless it is pre-cooked, in which case the time will be about the same as regular rice. Bulghur is rich in fiber and can be used in breads as well. If bulghur pilaf is leftover, you'll find that it is good even without reheating. Instead of having a sandwich for lunch, have a serving of leftover cracked wheat pilaf.

bulghur pilaf *serves 4*

1 onion, minced
¼ green pepper, minced
2 tbsp olive oil
2 cups bulghur
4 cups chicken broth
1 tbsp Worcestershire sauce
1 bay leaf
1 tbsp parsley
1 tsp dried basil
¼ cup chopped walnuts

Sauté onion and green pepper in oil in a heavy iron skillet over moderate heat. Add bulghur and cook 1 minute more. Add remaining ingredients and bring to a boil. Lower the heat and simmer about 30 minutes or until all the broth is absorbed. Serve.

Another famous Polish dish is golabki (pronounced gah-wum-key) or stuffed cabbage leaves. I tried to make it on one occasion but ran into some difficulties. Not wanting to throw away the ingredients, I came up with the following dish.

lazy golabki *serves 6*

3 cups cabbage, shredded
1 large onion, minced
1 tbsp olive oil
1 cup sauerkraut
2 lbs ground turkey
1 tbsp butter
2 cups cooked rice
28-oz tomato puree
½ cup water
1 tsp dried thyme
fresh ground pepper

Steam cabbage for 10 minutes. Sauté onion in olive oil for 3 minutes in an iron skillet over moderate heat. Add sauerkraut and cook for 5 minutes more, stirring occasionally. Remove to a small bowl. Cook ground turkey in butter in the skillet until completely browned. In a deep baking pan or casserole dish, layer half of the cabbage followed by half of the sauerkraut. Sprinkle meat on top and do the same with the rice. Spread remaining sauerkraut on top followed by the rest of the cabbage. Mix remaining ingredients and pour over the top. Bake in a 375° oven for 1 hour. Serve.

menu for day twenty-eight

bulghur pilaf
tossed salad
lazy golabki
fresh bread

The food at my first party was stuff I knew I could cook and tasted good. The recipe suggestions that follow are simple and also some of my early successes. The vegetable tray can have carrots, celery, broccoli, cauliflower, zucchini, cucumber and cherry tomatoes. The Russian dressing can be used for the dip.

The Russian dressing, the chowder and the baked beans can be made two days before. The bulghur pilaf, stewed hamburgers and Jell-O mold can be made the day before the party. Make one bread in the morning and the other in the afternoon along with the potato salad. The rest can be made just before the guests arrive. Once the party begins, turn on the oven and bake the chicken.

party number one

fish chowder
stewed hamburgers
Russian brown bread
hickory baked beans
vegetable Jell-O mold
bulghur pilaf
tasty baked chicken
onion rye bread
mixed vegetable tray
potato salad
Chinese cauliflower
fresh strawberries

One of the people I taught with in Binghamton became a good friend of mine. Fran taught business and was strict but fair and had a good sense of humor. One of his students named Maria was absent from school one day. As you may have guessed, she was Italian and it was not uncommon twenty years ago for Italian families to share in the chores of winemaking. Everyone had to do his or her part, no matter what age. Fran asked Maria where she had been the day before and her reply was that she had to stay home to help with making wine. To this Fran responded, "OK, let me see your feet!"

~~~~~~~~~~~~~~~~~~~~~~
~~~~~~~~~~~~~~~~~~~~~~

5. Upstate New York: grow it and keep it

My stay in New England was almost three years. In November 1983, I moved to Liverpool, New York and shortly thereafter, I bought a house in Plainville, the home of the turkey farm by the same name and not far from Syracuse. It was there that I grew corn for the first time. I had grown a few vegetables in the back yard of my first house, but that was a small area, with little sun. My new garden was to be four times as large with a greater variety of vegetables.

Some say that gardens are a lot of work and that may be true. However, the rewards are great. To begin with, gardening is very good for the mind as well as the body; it doesn't matter if your garden has vegetables or flowers in it. Over and above that, the resulting harvest of fruits and vegetables will be healthy (unless you load up on pesticides.) In addition to being healthy, the taste of your own produce will be unbelievable – you just can't beat it.

You can have a garden no matter where you live. In some areas you just won't be able to grow oranges, but don't feel bad. The places that grow the citrus can't grow other crops as well as you can grow in your area. Be resigned to growing what you can. There is an almost unlimited amount of things that you can harvest. Corn is not that hard to grow, but you need room and a great deal of sun. Tomatoes grow like weeds and there's nothing like a fresh tomato from the garden. Beans, cucumbers, peas, onions, lettuce and cabbage don't require that much effort. Beets, carrots and turnips are root vegetables that like sandy soil, but they are not that tough to grow.

My dad gave me some asparagus roots and plenty of seeds which I promptly planted in the fall of the first year. The roots give you asparagus the very next year, whereas it will take about three years to get asparagus from seeds.

However, once the crop starts to come in, it keeps on coming year after year. Twenty years is not unusual for one bed. As the asparagus shoots out of the ground in the spring, all you have to do is cut it, cook it and enjoy. You can harvest it every other day or so.

You can grow tomatoes from your own seeds if you start them indoors in March or April. You can also buy plants at the nursery since they are not that expensive. There you can buy three or more varieties of plants, such as beefsteak, cherry and plum. Beefsteak tomatoes take longer to grow but they store well; this means that you can have tomatoes long after the frost hits. There are quite a few varieties of cherry tomatoes, some very flavorful. Plum tomatoes are good for making spaghetti sauce since they are not very juicy. There are other kinds as well that are great tasting, too numerous to mention here. Just check a seed catalog and you can see the long list of varieties that are on the market today.

I have even grown okra, that necessary ingredient in Creole cooking, especially gumbos. I wound up with a good harvest not long ago whereas my first try in Plainville wasn't so plentiful. They do need a very hot climate in which to grow, hence the limited harvest. I also attempted to grow green peppers but with no luck for the same reason as the okra. What you can do is try vegetables and eliminate those that are not successful. That's what I did.

You can even grow herbs and spices. Chives, oregano and parsley are simple to grow and so are dill and mint. For other spices you will have to experiment on your own. At first, I never grew too many herbs, but with each season I try different ones. Spices in the store aren't that cheap, so it's a good idea to grow your own, if you can. They don't take up much space.

If you have a good-sized garden, you'll probably want to buy a freezer to keep what you can't eat right away.

Besides freezing stews and sauces, you can freeze vegetables right out of the garden. I had an abundant crop of tomatoes for a few years, so what I couldn't eat or give away, I froze. You can wash the tomatoes and put them in plastic bags into the freezer. When you're ready to use the tomatoes, thaw and the skins will come off quite easily (or so I've been told). I usually peel the tomatoes first and then freeze; this saves me the trouble of peeling them later. I also recommend not doing this with plum or cherry tomatoes. Since they are so small, you'll have a lot of work peeling them. The frozen tomatoes can be thawed and used in any recipe that calls for canned tomatoes, such as sauce, cacciatore, or jambalaya.

You can freeze just about any vegetable and fruit you like, even some herbs. Of course, some do better than others. Other vegetables store well so there is no need to freeze. This applies to bulbs, such as onions and garlic, roots such as potatoes, beets, carrots and turnips and squashes with hard shells, such as acorn and Hubbard.

To get started on your garden, you need to turn over the soil. I moved to Plainville in June so I had a tiny garden that first year. I turned over the soil by hand, or foot to be more precise. I used a long-handled shovel and though it took time, it was great exercise and it wasn't that bad. The year after that I decided on a much bigger enterprise and tried to find someone to plow the land. My neighbor Bob said he would do it. He did a nice job, but when I tried to pay him, he refused my offering and said a beer would do as payment. Now this was a good neighbor.

If you don't want to spade your garden by hand, you can find someone to plow your land. You could also buy or rent a Roto-tiller. That is probably the best way to do it. A hand cultivator can come in quite handy, not only for keeping the weeds down but also for loosening the soil in the early spring (once it has been plowed the year before). I spent a good deal of money for a hand cultivator that turned out to be a piece of junk. It just didn't work. My dad bought one many years ago and it lasted for years and years. That's the type to get. Unfortunately, they probably don't make that kind anymore.

As far as keeping the weeds down, there are different things you can do. My land in Plainville was surrounded by swamp on three sides and it seems the weeds kept seeding themselves in my garden. This can be a problem but keep it in perspective. After a time the crops will be so big that the weeds won't be a factor. You can use plastic to keep the weeds down as well as keep moisture in. Besides this, there are many methods used and being thought up to make your work in the garden easier. If you are creative, you will even come up with some.

You may have to worry about animals such as deer and raccoons. I had rabbits and raccoons but a fence took care of most of these little creatures. I even used the fence for cucumber vines to crawl onto, thus freeing up more space in the garden for other vegetables. It is amazing how one apparent problem turns into an advantage in another area. Above all, use manure and avoid poisons. After all, you are the one who will be eating the food. It's not like Uncle Ralph will be the only one to eat the stuff.

~~~~~~~~~~~
~~~~~~~~~~~

~~~ day twenty-nine ~~~

You may wonder if I ever poisoned anyone or if anyone got sick from my cooking. The answer is no – well, let me say that on one occasion something that ate my cooking died a short while after. It seems that if you live in the country, your home will either have a cat or there will be field mice in your house. I had one or two of the latter. In fact, I made some bread and this mouse (maybe it was a rat or Uncle Ernie) nibbled away at the bread. I didn't see the mouse at first, just the effect of his nibbling. I set a mousetrap with a little bait and before long I got him. Therefore, you could say that some creature partook of my cooking and eventually died.

Hong Kong chicken *serves 4*

2 tbsp olive oil
2 stalks celery, sliced
1 large onion, sliced
1 green pepper, sliced
1 can drained bamboo shoots
2 cups cooked chicken
¼ cup sherry
¼ cup soy sauce
1 tbsp grated ginger
2 tbsp brown sugar
2 tbsp cornstarch
8 oz tomato sauce

Heat the oil in a wok over high heat. Add celery, onion and green pepper and cook for 2 minutes. Add bamboo shoots and chicken and cook for 1 minute. Mix remaining ingredients in a small bowl and place in wok. Bring to a boil and simmer for 5 minutes. Serve over boiled rice.

stuffed mushrooms *serves 6*

3 slices of bacon	¼ cup walnuts, chopped
24 medium mushrooms	¼ cup sweet vermouth
1 small onion, minced	¼ tsp marjoram
¼ cup bread crumbs	fresh ground pepper

Sauté bacon in a large iron skillet over medium heat until crisp. Remove bacon to a paper towel to drain. Cut the stems off the mushrooms, chop finely and add with onion to the skillet. Cook until onion is transparent. Crumble bacon and add to the skillet along with bread crumbs, walnuts, vermouth, marjoram and pepper. Mix thoroughly and cook for 1 minute. Set mixture aside. Place mushroom caps open side down onto a cookie sheet and put under a warm broiler for 2 minutes. Turn mushrooms over and put back under broiler for 2 more minutes. Remove cookie sheet from the oven and stuff each mushroom with stuffing mixture. Place under broiler for 3 more minutes. Remove and serve.

menu for day twenty-nine

stuffed mushrooms	Hong Kong chicken
tossed salad	boiled rice
basil tomatoes	

~~~ day thirty ~~~

One of the great things about the seasons of the year is that each brings certain fruits and vegetables to eat. Late spring means fresh Bing cherries while August means fresh corn on the cob and homegrown tomatoes. I remember eating one tomato after another from the garden when I was a teenager. The taste was wonderful and my parents didn't mind. It would cost less to feed me that day. Who needs candy or ice cream anyway? I still feel the same way about fresh tomatoes today.

When a tomato, corn or any other vegetable is fresh from the garden, it needs no adornment. It is good just the way it is. If you pick corn yourself and cook it right away (now that is really fresh), it doesn't need butter or salt; it's perfection just as is, if it's cooked right. This is true of so many fruits and vegetables. Did you ever eat sweet peas out of the pod fresh from the garden? There is nothing like it.

If you have a few fresh juicy tomatoes and the summer heat is wearing you down, why make a hot meal when you can fix this spaghetti dish and the only thing you have to cook is the macaroni. Who said spaghetti sauce had to be hot to be good?

summer spaghetti *serves 4*

6 large tomatoes
4 tbsp olive oil
4 cloves garlic, minced
½ cup green olives, chopped
3 tbsp dried basil
fresh ground pepper
1 lb thin spaghetti

Quarter each tomato and slice as thinly as possible. Put into a glass bowl and add remaining ingredients, except for spaghetti. Toss well and store in a cool place for at least four hours, but not overnight. Avoid the refrigerator as the tomatoes will lose flavor there. Cook spaghetti according to package directions. Drain and put into a large bowl. Pour tomato sauce over spaghetti and toss. Serve.

You can cook corn inside on the stove with fine results, if the corn is fresh. But you can also roast the corn on a fire in its own husk. That's the way we did it as kids and it tasted so good. The corn has to soak a bit, and the cooking process actually involves steaming the corn. A wood fire is best and it takes a big fire. Pick the corn and soak it in a bucket of water for half an hour or so.

Once the fire is hot, remove the silk from the corn and place the ears (without shucking) on the fire. You will have to turn them every so often. The outer layer will be getting brown and before long the corn will be ready to eat. Just make sure you don't burn it.

corn on the cob *serves 6*

water
12 ears of corn

Bring a large pot of water to a boil. Shuck the corn and once water is boiling, place corn into the pot and return to a boil. Lower the heat and cook for 3 more minutes. Remove corn and serve.

cole slaw *serves 6*

1 small onion, thinly sliced
6 cups cabbage, shredded
2 carrots, grated
3 tbsp red wine vinegar
½ cup olive oil
2 tbsp caraway seeds
1 tbsp mustard seeds

Put onion, cabbage, carrots, and vinegar into a large bowl and toss well. Meanwhile heat olive oil in a small saucepan over moderate heat until oil is almost smoking. Add caraway seeds and mustard seeds and cook until mustard seeds are finished popping, about 2 minutes. Pour mustard mixture over cabbage and stir well. Refrigerate overnight. Serve.

menu for day thirty

corn on the cob
tossed salad
onion rye bread
summer spaghetti
cole slaw

~~~ day thirty-one ~~~

The last garden I had in Plainville was quite prolific. I bought some inexpensive seeds from the department store when they were on sale. Just because something is cheap doesn't mean it isn't good. I got green beans, carrots, beets and a few packets of cucumbers among others. I planted all the cucumbers and they really produced. I had more pickles than Heinz. There was a time when I was picking two eight-quart baskets every third day. They were quite good, but what do you do with all those cucumbers? I ate as much as I could, made some gazpacho, gave some to my family, froze some and made a few crocks of dills. My neighbor was the beneficiary of this abundance of cucumbers. That's what he gets for plowing my garden.

Polish dill pickles

6 sprigs of dill
2 dozen cucumbers, washed
12 cloves garlic, chopped
10 peppercorns
4 whole cloves
1 bay leaf
¼ cup sea salt
2 cups cider vinegar
boiling water

Place dill, cucumbers, garlic, peppercorns, cloves, bay leaf and sea salt into a crock or large jar. Pour vinegar over the mixture. Fill jar to the top with boiling water and set aside. The pickles should be ready in 1 or 2 weeks. Once they are ready, remove pickles and put in a container in the refrigerator.

beef and onions *serves 4*

2 lbs London broil
¼ cup soy sauce
2 tbsp olive oil
2 large onions, sliced thin
water
¼ cup dry sherry
3 tbsp cornstarch
egg noodles

Slice London broil into thin slivers and sprinkle 3 tablespoons of soy sauce on the meat. Marinate for 15 minutes. Heat oil in a wok over high heat and add the beef. Cook for 3 minutes. Add onions and cook 3 minutes more. Add the rest of the soy sauce, ½ cup of water and sherry and cook for 5 minutes. Mix cornstarch in ¼ cup of water and place in wok, while stirring. Cook until sauce thickens. Serve over boiled egg noodles.

steamed green beans *serves 4*

1 lb green beans
1 tbsp butter or margarine

Snap ends off the beans and wash. Place beans in a vegetable steamer and cook until they are tender, about 10 minutes. Place beans in a serving dish and add butter or margarine. Serve.

menu for day thirty-one

beef and onions
Polish dill pickles
corn on the cob
egg noodles
steamed green beans
basil tomatoes

~~~ day thirty-two ~~~

You can make creamy mustard dressing for salads by mixing mustard, mayonnaise and olive oil in a blender. I also throw in an extra ingredient or two for some added flavor. You can try different spices and seasonings in your recipe.

creamy mustard dressing *makes 1 cup*

3 tbsp Dijon mustard ½ cup mayonnaise
¼ cup olive oil
Put ingredients into a blender and mix until smooth, about 30 seconds. Refrigerate.

This next recipe combines the flavor of Polish sausage with the sauerkraut, wine and mustard of German cooking.

Viennese rice *serves 4*

1 small onion, minced
2 tbsp olive oil
2 cups white rice
½ cup sauerkraut
2 tbsp caraway seed
½ cup white wine
3 cups water
¼ lb smoked Polish sliced sausage
3 tbsp Dijon mustard
fresh ground pepper

Sauté onion in oil in a large iron skillet over medium heat. Add rice and cook for 1 minute. Add sauerkraut and cook for 2 minutes. Add caraway, wine, water, sausage and mustard and bring to a boil. Lower the heat and simmer until rice is cooked and water is absorbed, about 25 minutes. Add more water if necessary. Season with pepper and serve.

menu day thirty-two

Viennese rice
cooked broccoli
fresh bread
tossed salad with creamy mustard dressing

~~~ day thirty-three ~~~

I mentioned that you can freeze cucumbers, particularly those referred to as "bread and butter" pickles. You can even use glass jars for freezing; just make sure that you don't fill the jar all the way to the top. Plastic containers are fine too.

bread and butter pickles

2 quarts of cucumbers	½ cup vinegar
1 onion, thinly sliced	¼ tsp turmeric
1 tbsp sea salt	1 tbsp mustard seeds
1 cup sugar	

Slice the cucumbers very thin, 1/8 of an inch or less. Combine with the onion and salt and let stand overnight. The next day rinse the mixture and drain in a colander. Put remaining ingredients into a Dutch oven and bring to a boil. Lower the heat and continue stirring until sugar is completely dissolved. Add cucumber mixture to the Dutch oven and stir to blend. Let stand for 15 minutes. Put cucumbers into containers and freeze. The pickles can be thawed and eaten whenever you desire.

When I was young, I didn't care for mushrooms at all. Over the years, I have gotten to like them. I still am not a big fan of raw mushrooms in salads or on vegetable trays. This next recipe shows off that famous fungus in fine fashion.

chicken with mushrooms *serves 4*

1 chicken, cut up
5 tbsp of flour
2 tbsp olive oil
2 cloves garlic, minced
1 onion, chopped
½ lb sliced mushrooms
1 cup dry white wine
½ tsp dried thyme
1 cup chicken broth
¼ tsp dried tarragon
fresh ground pepper

Dredge the chicken in flour. Heat oil in a large Dutch oven and brown the chicken a few pieces at a time. Add garlic and onion and cook for 2 minutes. Add remaining ingredients and bring to a boil. Lower the heat and simmer until chicken is tender, about 40 minutes. Serve over rice.

menu for day thirty-three

chicken with mushrooms
basil tomatoes
cooked beets
rice pilaf
corn on the cob
bread and butter pickles

~~~ day thirty-four ~~~

I mentioned in chapter 1 that you can use ground turkey in place of ground beef in the recipe for chili. You could also use ground pork, or a combination of pork, beef and turkey. If you leave out the ground meat, you will have meatless chili and will hardly miss the meat.

three bean salad

1 can cut wax beans	½ cup sugar
1 can cut green beans	⅔ cup vinegar
1 can red kidney beans	½ cup olive oil
1 onion, thinly sliced	fresh ground pepper
1 green pepper, thinly sliced	

Drain the wax and green beans and put into a large glass bowl. Thoroughly wash the juice off the kidney beans and drain. Add kidney beans, onion and green pepper to the wax and green beans. In a small bowl, mix sugar and vinegar until sugar is dissolved. Add oil and stir in thoroughly. Add liquid and ground pepper to the beans and stir. Marinate for 24 hours. Serve.

menu for day thirty-four

meatless Chili	Cuban bread
tossed Salad	three bean salad
beer	boiled rice

~~~ day thirty-five ~~~

There are many types of fish that fall into different classes of taste and texture. Haddock and cod are similar in composition and taste. So are mussels and clams. Some fish are unique, such as tuna and salmon. Another fish in the same category as salmon and tuna is smelt. Despite the horrible sounding name (you could imply the same about scrod), smelts are delicious and easy to fix.

I recall a spring night when I was on the shore of Lake Erie with friends and the smelts were in season. The fish came out of the lake, onto the fire, and from there, into our mouths and stomachs. Add a beer or two and a little sauce, and it was quite a treat. I have bought frozen smelts and cooked them under the broiler and although you know they couldn't be quite as good as fresh out of the lake, they weren't bad. The bones are tiny so you can eat them or else the fish comes off the bones easily enough. Cooking time under the broiler is short indeed. Don't be turned off by the name "smelts."

broiled smelts *serves 2*

1 lb smelts
1 tbsp butter, melted
fresh ground pepper

Turn the oven broiler on. Place smelts in a shallow pan and brush with melted butter. Season with fresh ground pepper. Place the pan under the broiler until smelts are done, about 5 minutes. Make sure that they don't burn. Remove from the oven and serve.

German potato salad *serves 6*

3 lbs potatoes
¼ lb bacon, sliced
2 large onions, chopped
1 cup cider vinegar
½ cup white wine
3 Tbsp prepared mustard
sea salt to taste
fresh ground pepper

Wash potatoes and cut into quarters. Place them into a large Dutch oven, cover with water and bring to a boil. Lower the heat and cook until potatoes are 80% cooked, about 10 minutes or so. Drain potatoes and cool. Fry bacon and onions in a large iron skillet until onions are slightly soft and brown. Add vinegar, wine and mustard to the skillet and simmer for 5 minutes. When the potatoes have cooled down, slice them. In an ovenproof dish layer the potatoes, season with salt and pepper and put a layer of bacon and onion mix on top. Continue the layering process until the potatoes and onion/bacon mixture are gone. Cover with aluminum foil and bake at 325° for 1 hour. Remove from oven and serve.

menu for day thirty-five

broiled smelts
basil tomatoes
raisin rye bread
German potato salad
corn on the cob

A few years ago I had my annual corn roast in Plainville. Early in the morning on the day before the roast, I went out to check on the corn. From all indications, it seemed that it would be perfect and there would be plenty for everyone.

The next morning I went out to the garden and noticed many corn stalks sprawled out on the ground. The raccoons knew when the corn was to be ready and they had a feast. The year before I didn't have a problem because the farmer had planted corn behind my property and the raccoons had plenty and didn't have to attack my corn. This year he didn't plant corn as he let the land rest. I figure the raccoons were on the land before me so there wasn't too much I could do about it. Fortunately, I was able to pick enough corn for everyone to get a taste.

Now that we have some more new recipes and all those vegetables from the garden, we're ready for our second party: a corn roast.

party number two *(corn roast)*

gazpacho
corn on the cob
hot dogs and hamburgers
basil tomatoes
German potato salad
tossed salad
Cajun beans and rice
Polish dill pickles
stuffed mushrooms
grilled Italian sausage
raisin rye bread
three-bean salad
summer spaghetti
Hong Kong chicken
bread and butter pickles

During the last week of Lent, one of the songs that they use in the church is the Latin "Pange Lingua," which literally means, "Sing my tongue." During one such time, I attended the Holy Thursday celebration in New Canaan, Connecticut.

Just before the procession, the lector said, "our song will be found on page 343. It is 'Pange Linguini'." I thought to myself that that wasn't right. Then I realized it was. After all, it was the "Last Supper!"

~~~~~~~~~~~~~~~~~~~~~~
~~~~~~~~~~~~~~~~~~~~~~

6. The Gulf Coast: brunch time

I left upstate New York and moved to sunny Tampa, Florida. I didn't spend a great length of time there and missed out on the grueling summer heat. This was not my first trip to the Sunshine state. My first time was during Easter vacation of my first or second year of teaching. Two of my friends and I drove down to Tampa / St. Petersburg and stayed with one of their relatives. We eventually made our way to Pompano Beach and camped out for a few days. Since then I have been in the state on numerous vacation trips.

What better place to have brunch than in sunny Florida? If you miss breakfast and it's close to lunchtime, why not brunch? Of course, you shouldn't miss breakfast, as it is the most important meal of the day. Nothing compares to steak and eggs, even though it may not be good for you. You can have it on occasion and the same can be said for eggs served by themselves or with bacon, sausage or ham. Moderation is the key to good health and happiness.

There is nothing wrong with cereal, toast and juice for your morning meal. I use low-fat milk on my cereal and avoid cereals with sugar and high-sodium content. Shredded wheat and puffed wheat are virtually salt-free, sodium-free and good for you. You can add fruit such as bananas or fresh strawberries for excitement. As far as toast, I prefer a rye or wheat bread with orange marmalade or some type of jam. Butter or margarine as an occasional indulgence is fine.

Another good option is fresh grapefruit, and juice is loaded with plenty of vitamins, no matter what your preference. I enjoy a cup of fresh brewed coffee every so often with neither sugar nor cream. You can add a half-teaspoon of cinnamon to the coffee as it is brewing for a pleasant change of pace. There are quite a few choices of exotic blends of coffee at your local supermarket, such as raspberry chocolate or amaretto decaf.

There is no reason why you have to limit your breakfast to the usual fare of the morning. I know many people who love cold pizza for breakfast or leftover Chinese courses. If you really consider it, the largest meal of the day should be breakfast, with lunch a bit less and dinner the lightest meal of the day. And yet, we all know people who have their largest meal of the day at nine o'clock at night.

Brunch makes a lot of sense. The kind that doesn't emphasize bacon, sausage, ham and eggs is best. In other words, a buffet is the way to go, with the less fat and cholesterol, the better. When I was younger, my mother always prepared the largest meal of the day on Sunday at one in the afternoon. Many people still do this and we should all do the same not only on the Sabbath but also on the other days of the week.

Speaking of days past, I recall summers as a teenager working on a farm not far from my parents' home. My lunch was prepared by my mother, and it was huge. As far as I can recall it consisted of two sandwiches, some cookies and / or cake, a can of pop (soda if you're from New York

City or close by), a banana, orange, tomato, pear and a candy bar. That was a heck of a lunch. I always finished it, though.

Currently I fix my own lunch and it consists mainly of fruit and vegetables, with an occasional cookie, dried fruit or sandwich. Occasionally, I would even use the microwave at work to heat a leftover soup or casserole. My lunch can be quite large at times but never unhealthy. Of course, I do go out to lunch every so often.

~~~~~~~~~~~
~~~~~~~~~~~

~~~ day thirty-six ~~~

Chicken dishes are great for parties because you can make them a day ahead and just warm up when needed. The day in the refrigerator may even help blend the flavors better. You can even freeze them far in advance, once they're cooked. This chicken dish features a rum and soy sauce marinade. You can simmer it on top of the stove if you prefer, rather than baking in the oven.

rum chicken *serves 4*

1 chicken, cut up
2 tbsp lime juice
⅓ cup soy sauce
½ cup rum
4 tbsp flour
3 tbsp olive oil
3 large onions, chopped
¼ tsp dried tarragon

Marinate chicken pieces in lime juice, soy sauce and rum overnight. Remove chicken from marinade and reserve marinade. Place flour into a plastic bag and dredge chicken with the flour. Heat olive oil in a heavy iron skillet and brown the chicken, a few pieces at a time. Remove the browned pieces to a large ovenproof casserole dish. Add chopped onions, tarragon and marinade, cover and bake in a 350° oven for 1 hour or until chicken is tender. Serve over egg noodles or boiled rice.

boiled brussels sprouts *serves 4*

1 pint brussels sprouts	2 tbsp butter
1 cup water	fresh ground pepper

Clean the sprouts and place in a small saucepan with the water. Bring to a boil, lower the heat, and cook until tender, about 10 minutes. Drain brussels sprouts; add the butter and season with fresh ground pepper. Serve.

I have made the following dressing on numerous occasions and it seems that it tastes slightly different each time. This has to do with the sesame seeds, which can be toasted lightly or used as is. Keep an eye on the sesame seeds as you brown them, since they tend to burn rather easily. Burnt sesame dressing won't be a hit with too many people. I have also used this dressing as a dip for raw vegetables.

sesame dressing *makes 2 cups*

1 cup canola oil	fresh grated ginger
½ tsp sugar	½ stalk of celery
2 tbsp chopped onion	¼ cup toasted sesame seeds
¼ tsp celery seeds	¼ cup soy sauce
fresh ground pepper	⅓ cup white vinegar

Place all ingredients except soy sauce and vinegar into a blender and blend for 30 seconds. Add soy sauce and vinegar and blend for 30 seconds more. Store in the refrigerator.

A frequent diet of bacon is not recommended but bacon does add a zest to many foods, even a small amount. As I mentioned earlier, store bacon in the freezer for easier slicing. You'll also forget about it and eat less of it as well.

horseradish mushrooms *serves 4*

3 slices bacon	snipped fresh chives
1 tbsp butter	2 tbsp horseradish
2 tbsp olive oil	¼ tsp cayenne pepper
1 lb mushrooms	

If the bacon is frozen, slice off the equivalent of 3 slices of bacon into ¼-inch pieces or smaller. Sauté bacon in a large iron skillet until crisp. Remove from skillet to paper towels. Crumble the bacon if necessary and set aside. Pour bacon fat off the skillet, melt butter, and add olive oil. Cut mushrooms in half and sauté until they are tender, about 5 minutes. Remove mushrooms to a small dish. Add chives, horseradish and cayenne pepper to the skillet and simmer for 1 minute, stirring occasionally. Add mushrooms and bacon and simmer for 1 minute more to blend in the flavors. Remove and serve.

menu for day thirty-six

horseradish mushrooms rum chicken
boiled brussels sprouts egg noodles
tossed salad with sesame dressing

~~~ day thirty-seven ~~~

Meat adds so much flavor to spaghetti sauce, whether it be pork, beef or chicken. However, fresh spices and vegetables can create a heavenly sauce too, as exemplified by the summer spaghetti in the last chapter. This sauce wasn't even cooked either. One meatless sauce I shall never forget was one I enjoyed in Wales on a summer vacation in Europe. I couldn't even tell you all the ingredients, but I am sure that they included fresh herbs with fresh tomatoes. This sauce was cooked and it seemed to get better with each mouthful.

I doubt that I'll ever duplicate that recipe but here is a recipe that I hope will suffice.

meatless spaghetti *serves 4*

½ cup olive oil ½ tsp sugar
4 cloves garlic, minced pinch dried red pepper
5 large tomatoes, peeled and chopped
handful fresh basil leaves 1 lb thin spaghetti

Add olive oil to a heavy iron skillet on moderate heat. Add garlic and cook until golden brown. Add tomatoes, 1 at a time. Add basil, sugar and red pepper and cook about 15 more minutes. Meanwhile cook the spaghetti "al dente", about 8 minutes. Drain the spaghetti and add to the skillet. Mix the sauce and spaghetti while still simmering for about 1 minute more. Serve.

Chicken wings make a great appetizer and taste good cold as leftovers. Buffalo wings originated in the Anchor Bar in downtown Buffalo a few years ago and can now be found all the way across the nation. I have never made Buffalo wings but have eaten my share of them. This recipe has gotten raves from those who have tried it.

Chinese chicken wings *serves 6*

4 tbsp brown sugar
½ tbsp sesame oil
⅓ cup soy sauce
fresh grated ginger
2 cloves garlic, minced
¼ tsp ground cinnamon
½ cup Sherry vermouth
dash of hot oil
24 chicken wings

Mix all ingredients together except for the wings. Place wings in a large glass bowl and add marinade. Let wings marinate overnight, if not longer. The longer they marinate, the better the flavor. Bake wings in a 400° oven until tender, about 35 minutes. Serve.

menu for day thirty-seven

Chinese chicken wings
Cuban bread
meatless spaghetti
tossed salad

~~~ day thirty-eight ~~~

Shrimp makes an excellent appetizer. Its only drawback is the cost. However, if you splurge, you'll find that it's worth it. Marinated shrimp should be done a day ahead of time so that the flavors blend in. That means less preparation on the day of your dinner. This recipe is simple but you'll have to cook it just before you serve it. Just one word of caution: don't overcook shrimp, unless you like chewing and chewing and chewing.

dilled shrimp *serves 4*

2 tbsp olive oil
3 tbsp butter
snipped fresh dill
1 lb shelled large shrimp
2 tbsp lemon juice
fresh ground pepper
¼ tsp Tabasco sauce
1 tsp Worcestershire sauce

In a large iron skillet, heat olive oil, butter, and dill over moderate heat. Add shrimp and cook until it is pink, about 2 minutes. Add remaining ingredients and simmer for 1 minute more. Remove from skillet and serve.

Picadillo can be served in tacos or over rice. You can make it with beef or pork, but the following recipe calls for ground turkey. You can make it with any of these meats or with a mix if you like.

picadillo *serves 4*

3 tbsp olive oil
1 large onion, chopped
2 cloves garlic, minced
1 green pepper, chopped
¼ cup sliced almonds
1 lb ground turkey
6 oz tomato paste
1½ tbsp vinegar
2 tbsp ground cumin
1 tsp dried oregano
1 tbsp Tabasco sauce
1 bay leaf
1 cup sweet vermouth
1 cup water
½ cup green chopped olives
fresh ground pepper

In a heavy iron skillet, heat oil over moderate heat. Add onion and simmer until softened. Add garlic, green pepper, and almonds and cook for about 5 minutes. Add ground meat and cook until browned, about 6 minutes. Add remaining ingredients and bring to a boil. Simmer for 45 minutes. Serve over boiled rice.

The following recipe can use peaches in place of the nectarines, without losing flavor.

Oriental nectarine slaw *serves 6*

½ cup mayonnaise
1 tbsp soy sauce
2 tbsp white vinegar
1 stalk celery, minced
2 cups cabbage, shredded
2 cups cooked turkey, chopped
fresh ground ginger
fresh ground pepper
1 small onion, minced
4 nectarines, diced

In a small bowl, mix the mayonnaise, soy sauce and vinegar until they are well blended. Mix remaining ingredients in a large bowl and add the mayonnaise mixture. Blend well and refrigerate overnight. Serve.

menu for day thirty-eight

dilled shrimp
boiled rice
Oriental nectarine slaw
picadillo
steamed vegetables

~~~ day thirty-nine ~~~

Another favorite food in Western New York is beef on weck, also known as roast beef on kimmelweck. The roast beef is covered with gravy and served on a roll called kimmelweck, which is nothing more than a hard roll covered in salt. We can get rid of the sodium by using a hard roll sans salt. If you have beef left over from your roast of beef, slice it and warm up some of the beef gravy. If there is no gravy, you can always have beef without it or warm some French onion soup for dipping the rolls. Believe it or not, onion soup is quite easy to make and certainly worth the effort. The hardest part is slicing the onions.

French onion soup *serves 8*

2 tbsp butter
1 tbsp olive oil
5 onions, very thinly sliced
3 beef bouillon cubes
3 quarts of water
1 tsp sugar
3 tbsp flour
1 cup dry white wine
1 small bay leaf
fresh ground pepper
½ cup brandy
bread croutons
sliced Swiss cheese

Put butter and olive oil into a heavy iron skillet on low heat. When butter is melted, add onions, cover, and cook for 30 minutes. Meanwhile, put bouillon and water into a large pot and bring to a boil. Lower the heat to simmer. When a half hour has elapsed for the onions, raise the heat to moderate and add sugar. The sugar helps the onions to brown. Stir occasionally and continue cooking until onions are golden brown. Add flour and cook for 3 minutes, stirring as necessary. Add onions to the simmering stock along with the wine, bay leaf and pepper and simmer over low heat for 1 hour. Add brandy and heat through. Remove from the stove and refrigerate. Make the bread croutons by slicing Italian or French bread ½ inch thick. Put them on a cookie sheet in a 325° oven and bake until they are golden brown. Check occasionally to keep them from burning and remove them from the oven when done. To serve the onion soup, heat up and pour the soup into separate bowls over 1 crouton each. If cheese is desired, use ovenproof bowls and place a slice of cheese on top of each crouton and place under the oven broiler until the cheese is melted, about 5 minutes.

Russian potato salad *serves 6*

5 large potatoes
6 radishes, sliced
3 dill pickles, sliced
1 cup Russian dressing

Wash the potatoes and quarter each. Place in a large pot and add water to cover. Cook until potatoes are soft, about twenty minutes. Drain and cool. When cool, cube potatoes and put into a large bowl, add remaining ingredients and stir. Refrigerate overnight. Serve.

menu for day thirty-nine

roast beef on hard roll
French onion soup
Russian potato salad
hickory baked beans
Polish dill pickles

~~~ day forty ~~~

As far as curry goes, you either like it or you hate it. One of the most flavorful and delicious meals I have ever had from an Indian restaurant was take-out. It was during a vacation in England a few years ago. A former classmate of mine living there ordered us a variety of Indian dishes and I will never forget the different flavors of curry present. I'm sure the English are thankful for the Italian, Indian and Hungarian restaurants in their country, as most English food is rather bland.

I once made a dish of beef curry which I wasn't thrilled with, even though my guests liked it. I probably won't ever make beef curry again. I will make chicken curry though. I think you'll like this recipe too.

chicken curry *serves 4*

rind of ½ lemon
3 tbsp olive oil
2 cloves garlic, minced
2 large onions, chopped
½ tbsp ground turmeric
¼ tsp nutmeg
1 tbsp ground coriander
½ tsp ground cumin
fresh ground ginger
fresh ground pepper
1 chicken, cut up
1 large tomato, peeled and chopped
½ head cauliflower, cut into flowerets

Put lemon rind, oil, garlic, and onions into a blender and puree into a paste. In a large Dutch oven cook paste over moderate heat for 4 minutes, add remaining spices, and cook for 1 minute. Put chicken into the pot and coat each piece well with the mix. Cook for 30 minutes over low heat. Stir in tomato and cauliflower and simmer for 20 minutes more. Serve over boiled rice.

Meatballs make a good appetizer, can be made ahead of time and can even be frozen. You can warm them in a crock-pot if you have one and thus eliminate worries about what pot to use for reheating. The recipe for meatballs from an earlier chapter can be modified as an appetizer by just making the meatballs tinier. The same sauce can be used or you may want to try a variation. The following recipe pleased many palates at my place recently.

sweet and sour meatballs *serves 6*

1 lb lean ground beef
½ cup rye bread crumbs
1 egg, scrambled
1 tsp dried basil
fresh ground pepper
¼ tsp dried thyme
1 onion, finely minced
3 tbsp olive oil
¼ cup Dijon mustard
½ cup ketchup
3 tbsp molasses
¼ cup wine vinegar

In a large bowl, combine ground beef, bread crumbs, egg, basil, pepper, thyme, and onion. Mix thoroughly and form into tiny meatballs. In a heavy iron skillet, heat olive oil over medium heat and brown meatballs, a few at a time on all sides. Remove to a Dutch oven when browned. In a small bowl mix the mustard, ketchup, molasses, and vinegar and pour over the meatballs. Simmer meatballs for 35 minutes. Remove and serve with toothpicks.

menu for day forty

sweet and sour meatballs
boiled rice
spicy applesauce
chicken curry
escarole orange salad

~~~ day forty-one ~~~

Being of Polish descent, I am no stranger to pierogi. My mother makes them quite frequently and my friend Bill has prepared them on occasion. As far as I am concerned, it's just too much work to make your own. However, I have made a dish that incorporates the flavor and the ingredients of pierogi. It is a simple casserole and it is called "lazy pierogi." The left over gravy that it calls for can be from chicken, pork, or beef. They are all acceptable.

lazy pierogi *serves 8*

1 clove garlic, minced
1 large onion, chopped
1 tbsp olive oil
1-lb can sauerkraut
fresh ground pepper
½ lb mushrooms, sliced
leftover gravy
½ cup dry white wine
1 lb spiral macaroni

In a heavy iron skillet, sauté garlic and onion in oil over medium heat for 3 minutes. Add sauerkraut and pepper and simmer slowly for 10 more minutes. Add mushrooms and simmer for 5 minutes more. Add gravy and wine and heat through, stirring to blend all ingredients. Meanwhile cook macaroni according to the directions on package. In an ovenproof casserole dish, mix the macaroni and sauerkraut mixture and place in a 350° oven. Bake for ½ hour. This can be cooked in a Dutch oven on the stove as well. Serve.

Gumbo file is essential in gumbo dishes and it is basically nothing more than ground sassafras leaves. You can find it in specialty shops and large supermarkets. It adds a wonderful zest to dishes.

Creole shrimp *serves 4*

3 tbsp red wine vinegar
1 tsp lime juice
2 tsp Dijon mustard
⅓ cup olive oil
1 tsp Worcestershire sauce
1 celery stalk, minced
2 tbsp Creole seasoning
1 tsp gumbo file
1 lb cooked shrimp

In a small bowl, mix vinegar, lime juice and mustard and add oil in a stream, mixing thoroughly. Add the remaining ingredients and mix well. Pour over shrimp and marinate overnight. Serve with toothpicks.

You may have noticed that quite a few of my recipes call for a pinch of cayenne pepper. There is a reason why I use only a pinch. It's fiery hot stuff. Just remember that you can always add more of a hot spice, but I am not sure what you can do to cool it down if it's too hot.

Creole seasoning

3 tbsp paprika
cayenne pepper
1 tbsp dried oregano
2 tbsp fresh ground pepper
2 tbsp garlic powder
1 tbsp dried thyme
1 tbsp onion powder

In a small bowl, mix all the ingredients. Transfer to a small jar and store in a cool, dry place.

picnic cole slaw *serves 8*

1 head of cabbage
1 large onion, sliced
1 green pepper, sliced
1 cup sliced green olives
½ cup sugar
¾ cup white vinegar
½ cup olive oil
1 tsp Dijon mustard
1 tsp celery seeds

Thinly slice cabbage, onion and green pepper. Combine with olives in a large bowl. In a small saucepan, combine remaining ingredients. Bring to a boil and simmer for 5 minutes, stirring occasionally. Pour over the vegetables and thoroughly mix. Refrigerate overnight and serve.

If you don't have a waffle iron, you'll have to skip this next recipe. I received one as a gift quite a few years ago. Even though it is a luxury kitchen item, mine has gotten a great deal of use over the years. You will need an electric mixer for this recipe as well, but it will come in handy on numerous occasions. The secret to this recipe is the beating of the egg whites separately from the yolks.

cinnamon walnut waffles *serves 4*

non-stick cooking spray
2 eggs, separated
1½ cups milk
⅓ cup olive oil
1¾ cups flour
1 tbsp sugar
1 tbsp cinnamon
1 tbsp baking powder
pinch of salt
¼ cup walnuts, finely chopped

Heat waffle iron after spraying both sides with the cooking spray. In a small bowl beat egg whites until stiff. In a large bowl, beat egg yolks until they lighten in color. Add milk and oil and continue beating for 30 seconds. Add dry ingredients and continue mixing until thoroughly blended. Blend in walnuts and egg whites by hand. Pour 1 cup of the mix at a time onto waffle iron and cook until golden brown. Repeat until waffles are cooked. Serve the waffles with blueberry or maple syrup.

menu for day forty-one

cinnamon walnut waffles
lazy pierogi
dilled carrots
Creole shrimp
picnic cole slaw

~~~ day forty-two ~~~

Some combinations of food sound unappetizing and perhaps rightly so. I once cooked a fettuccine made with peanut butter. I didn't like it. In fact, I will never combine peanuts with any main dish I cook, and I must say I like peanuts. Another combination that may not sound very appealing is pork with prunes. You just have to try it before passing judgment. That won't be the only thing you'll pass!

pork with prunes *serves 4*

2 lbs lean pork stew
4 tbsp flour
2 tbsp olive oil
fresh ground pepper
fresh ground ginger
2 cups dry white wine
½ cup water
10 pitted prunes

Dredge pork cubes in flour. Heat oil in a Dutch oven and brown pork over moderate heat with pepper and ginger. Add remaining ingredients and simmer over very low heat for 1½ hours. Refrigerate overnight and reheat the next day. Serve over egg noodles.

mustard caraway wings *serves 6*

¼ cup mayonnaise
3 tbsp cider vinegar
¼ cup Dijon mustard
24 chicken wings
1 tbsp caraway seeds
2 cups rye bread crumbs

In a large bowl, combine mayonnaise, vinegar and mustard. Put wings into the bowl and mix to coat. Refrigerate overnight. The next day crush the caraway seeds in a mortar and pestle and mix into the bread crumbs. Dip wings into the crumb mixture and place on a rack over a cookie sheet. Bake in a 450° oven until golden brown, about 40 minutes. Serve.

menu for day forty-two

mustard caraway wings
egg noodles
Chinese cabbage
pork with prunes
tossed salad

party number three

Spanish chicken wings
dilled shrimp
biscotti
Oriental nectarine slaw
spicy applesauce
Russian potato salad
stuffed mushrooms
Polish dill pickles
cinnamon raisin bread
roast loin of pork
lazy pierogi
steamed vegetables
vegetable tray with sesame dressing

I had some friends over from work for dinner some time ago. I made some French onion soup and commented that the hardest part was slicing the onions. One of the consequences was that the eyes tend to fill with tears from the onions. Frank, being the perfect straight man, mentioned that he heard that peeling onions underwater was supposed to help. I said, “I tried that but I almost drowned.”

~~~~~~~~~~~~~~~~~~~~~~
~~~~~~~~~~~~~~~~~~~~~~

7. Back to Westchester: camping and tailgating

I returned to the north within a short stretch of time. Travel brings to mind camping and cookouts in the great outdoors. You can certainly cook on a fire, using charcoal, wood or even gas, as now portable gas grills are available. A Coleman stove can almost simulate cooking in your kitchen, minus the oven, of course.

I will never forget one camping trip into eastern Canada and Maine a few years back. We made our own oven outdoors and baked a chicken. We used large rocks, aluminum foil and plenty of charcoal. We spread bacon grease on the chicken and wrapped it in foil. It was superb and it took only twenty minutes to complete. I wouldn't say the fire was hot but some of the foil melted (not around the chicken). We had our own microwave.

My late uncle Dick would cook a small turkey outdoors on the grill. He did a good job of it. I have been to goat roasts and pig roasts and I'm sure you have too. The possibilities are almost endless as to what you can cook outdoors. You're only limited by your imagination.

If you are fortunate to have a Coleman stove, you can cook just about anything outdoors. On many occasions, I have prepared dishes ahead and just warmed them the day we ate them. Here is an even better idea. Why not make French onion soup and freeze it in a square container. As it is thawing in the cooler, the soup can serve as your ice. You can also do the same with chili, casseroles, and cut up chicken. It just will require you to know when the item will be completely thawed, but that is something you can live with.

As you can imagine, I have never gone hungry on a camping trip or at a tailgating party before or after a football game. The foods that we have eaten are as varied as the recipes in this book. We had chili for one Thanksgiving dinner during a camping trip in Great Smoky Mountain National Park of Tennessee. I made sauerbraten with egg noodles and sweet and sour red cabbage for one tailgate party a few years ago. Why not do it right?

~~~ day forty-three ~~~

The secret to marinating and basting is to let the food marinate long enough to eliminate the need to baste. This applies to meat as well as fish. A few years ago for the Dolphins versus Bills game at Rich Stadium, I had to settle for swordfish since I couldn't find any dolphin. I have eaten the latter before and it is delicious. By the way, I don't cook horse when the Bills play the Colts.

The marinade for the swordfish smelled so heavenly, that all I had to do was to grill it. The fire was just right so I put the steaks on the grill. They cooked beautifully and were ready to be removed when my friend Bill suggested I pour the remaining marinade onto the fish just before taking them off the grill. It added a trifle amount of flavor to the swordfish. The big bonus was how the outdoors was permeated with the brilliant marinade aroma.

marinated swordfish *serves 4*

4 medium swordfish steaks
4 tbsp soy sauce
fresh grated ginger
1 tsp grated orange peel
½ cup olive oil
½ cup sherry
2 tsp dill weed

Place swordfish in a glass bowl. In a small bowl mix remaining ingredients and pour over fish. Let marinate overnight. Place steaks on a hot charcoal fire and cook each side approximately 7 minutes. This will depend on the thickness of the steaks and the intensity of the fire. Remove and serve.

This next recipe may seem a little contradictory: Indian beans using French-style green beans. Trust me – it's an international dish.

Indian green beans *serves 4*

1 tbsp butter
1 tbsp olive oil
1 tsp mustard seeds
1 small onion, minced
fresh grated ginger
2 tsp ground coriander
½ tsp ground cumin
10 oz French-style green beans
2 tbsp lemon juice

In a heavy iron skillet on medium heat, melt butter with oil. Add mustard seeds and sauté until they begin to pop, about ½ minute. Add onion, ginger, coriander, and cumin and cook until onion is soft. Add green beans and lemon juice and continue simmering for 3 minutes. Serve.

boiled cabbage *serves 4*

1 head of cabbage
2 cups of water
fresh ground pepper
2 tbsp butter

Trim the outside leaves of the cabbage and quarter. Put cabbage into a medium saucepan and add water. Bring to a boil and simmer until tender, about 10 minutes. Drain; add the pepper and butter, if desired. Serve.

menu for day forty-three

marinated swordfish
rice pilaf
vegetable tray with Russian dip
boiled cabbage
Indian green beans

~~~ day forty-four ~~~

I mentioned that chicken is quite versatile and difficult to mess up. This brings to mind a day in Albany when I volunteered to make the barbeque sauce for the chicken at a friend's house. I had my own recipe that was good so I wasn't worried. Unfortunately, it seemed that as I went down the list of my required ingredients for the sauce, one after another was missing and no one felt like driving to town to get them. So I improvised and mixed something together. I really don't recall exactly what went into it. The sauce didn't smell great, but we slopped it on the chicken anyway and the chicken was very good. You just never know.

The chicken can be parboiled if you like. If not, be sure to cut the chicken into small pieces to assure that no piece is partially cooked. Chicken tartare is about as popular as chicken salmonella.

tangy barbequed chicken *serves 4*

1 chicken, cut up	tangy barbeque sauce

Place the chicken on a hot fire and cook the first side for about 20 minutes. After turning the chicken, spread sauce on the top and cook the second side 20 minutes. Turn the chicken oven and spread sauce on the second side. Continue cooking and basting until the chicken is thoroughly cooked. Remove the chicken and if any piece is not properly cooked, return to the grill for a few more minutes.

tangy barbeque sauce *for 2 chickens*

6 pitted prunes
1 tbsp hot chili paste
3 tbsp olive oil
⅓ cup lemon juice
1 tbsp Worcestershire sauce
8 oz tomato sauce
1 large onion, minced
2 cloves garlic, minced
1 tbsp dry mustard

Put the prunes, chili paste, oil, juice, Worcestershire sauce and tomato sauce into a blender and puree. Add the remaining ingredients and puree for 30 seconds more. Transfer the sauce to a small saucepan and simmer for ½ hour, stirring occasionally. Refrigerate until ready to use.

menu for day forty-four

tasty barbequed chicken
German potato salad
tossed salad
garlic cauliflower
Polish dill pickles

~~~ day forty-five ~~~

You need not buy salad dressing from the supermarket. Make your own. The stores today sell all different kinds of vinegars and you can experiment. Not too long ago I bought a bottle of raspberry flavored vinegar and the back of the bottle had a recipe for dressing. I tried it and it was very good. True French dressing is vinegar and oil. The recipe that follows is a tomato French dressing. If this is too sweet for you, reduce the amount of sugar. If not sweet enough, add some.

French dressing *makes 3 cups*

¾ cup olive oil	¾ cup vinegar
¼ cup sugar	¾ cup ketchup
½ tbsp garlic powder	1 small onion, minced
½ tbsp celery seeds	½ tsp Worcestershire sauce
½ tsp dry mustard	1 tsp paprika

Put all the ingredients into a blender and puree. Refrigerate.

Between Christmas and New Year's Day a few years ago, I invited some relatives over for dinner. Not as many people sat down to dinner as I had planned. I made fruit Jell-O mold and my Aunt Esther brought a raspberry applesauce Jell-O dish, unknown to me until her arrival. The children may not have eaten too much of the other food I prepared, but they made sure that the Jell-O was not left over. Here is my version of fruit Jell-O.

Jell-O fruit mold *serves 6*

1 package Jell-O
2 cups of water
16 oz fruit cocktail
1 cup tiny marshmallows
½ cup chopped walnuts

Prepare the Jell-O according to the package directions. Refrigerate until the Jell-O begins to set, about 30 minutes. Drain the fruit cocktail. If you don't want to use the canned variety, use fresh fruit, such as oranges, pineapple, peaches, pears, seedless grapes, and grapefruit. In a large bowl, mix the fruit, marshmallows, walnuts, and semi-set Jell-O. Pour into a Jell-O mold and refrigerate overnight. Unmold by dipping in warm water. Serve.

There is nothing like Polish sausage, and that includes the fresh variety as well as the more familiar kind found in any supermarket, the smoked variety. You will really have to search to find fresh Polish sausage unless you live in a city with a large Polish population such as Buffalo, Chicago, or Milwaukee. You can ask at the butcher shop or else make your own. Each variety offers a different flavor to any dish and you can use either or both kinds in the following soup recipe even though it calls for fresh Polish sausage.

lentil sausage soup *serves 8*

1 ham hock
2 cups lentils
7 cups water
1 bay leaf
½ tsp dried thyme
½ tsp salt
16-oz can tomatoes
pinch of sugar
3 stalks celery, chopped
2 carrots, chopped
large onion, chopped
1 clove garlic, minced
¼ lb fresh cooked Polish sausage
½ cup ditalini
fresh ground pepper

Place the ham hock, lentils, water, bay leaf, and thyme into a large Dutch oven and bring to a boil. Lower the heat and simmer for 1 hour. Add the salt, tomatoes, sugar, celery, carrots, onion, and garlic and simmer for 20 minutes more. Slice the Polish sausage ¼ inch or less, add to the soup and continue simmering until the vegetables are tender, about 10 minutes. Remove the ham hock and let cool. Add the ditalini and simmer until done. Separate any meat from the ham hock and add back to the soup with the ground pepper. Refrigerate overnight. Warm and serve.

menu for day forty-five

lentil sausage soup
French bread
Jell-O fruit mold
steamed green beans
tossed salad with French dressing

~~~ day forty-six ~~~

I don't usually use dips for chips and vegetables, except for an occasional salsa. That's because most dips are loaded with calories, fat, and cholesterol. However, salsas and bean dips certainly don't fit into the same category. Hummus is another healthy dip that you can use. If you're familiar with Middle Eastern cooking, then you probably have heard of tabbouleh, hummus, pita bread, stuffed grape leaves and kibbeh. I dated a Lebanese woman a few years ago. I was at her parents' home on many occasions. Her mother loved to cook, so I experienced the cuisine of that part of the world. I can't honestly say that Middle Eastern food is one of my favorites. Fortunately, this family had Cuban influences so that made for some great dinners.

Here is a recipe for lentil hummus that is great for dipping raw vegetables or bread.

lentil hummus *serves 8*

1 cup lentils
4 cloves garlic, minced
1 small onion, minced
4 cups water
1 clove
5 sprigs parsley
1 bay leaf
¼ tsp dried thyme
1 chicken bouillon cube
⅓ cup lemon juice
¼ cup olive oil
½ cup tahini
¼ tsp cayenne pepper
fresh ground pepper

In a large pan put lentils, 2 cloves of garlic, onion, water, clove, parsley, bay leaf, thyme, and bouillon cube. Bring to a boil and simmer until lentils are tender, about 45 minutes. Drain the lentils and cool. Remove the bay leaf and clove, if you can find it and puree the lentils in a blender. Add remaining garlic and lemon juice and puree. Transfer mixture to a large bowl and blend in the olive oil, tahini, cayenne pepper, and black pepper. Hummus may be refrigerated. Serve.

Fresh asparagus from the garden is good when steamed for a few minutes. Nothing needs to be added. I prefer it slightly crunchy.

steamed asparagus *serves 4*

1 lb asparagus
water

Trim the ends and wash each stalk. Place asparagus in the water in a shallow pan and cook until tender, about 4 minutes. Serve.

I mentioned the famous speedie of Binghamton. Someday I will come up with the recipe for that specialty. For now, this will have to do.

marinated pork *serves 4*

½ tsp ground marjoram
¼ cup sherry
2 tbsp honey
2 garlic cloves, minced
1 tsp dried thyme
1 bay leaf, crumbled
⅓ cup olive oil
2 tbsp soy sauce
2 tbsp lemon juice
1 tsp dried sage
2 lbs lean pork stew
metal skewers

Thoroughly combine all ingredients, except for the pork. Pour marinade over pork and refrigerate overnight. Thread about 5 pieces of pork on each metal skewer and cook over hot charcoal, turning until pork is cooked through. When pork is done, wrap a thin slice of Italian bread around it, and pull meat off the skewer. Indulge.

menu for day forty-six

marinated pork
lentil hummus
sliced Italian bread
steamed asparagus
vegetable tray with sesame dressing

~~~ day forty-seven ~~~

Monkfish brings with it a texture similar to that of lobster. If you have ever had lobster in a restaurant in some kind of dish, you may wonder if you weren't actually eating lobster, but monkfish. A few years ago, I met some friends for lunch and each of us had the specialty of the restaurant, lobster bisque. It was very good and not cheap. I sincerely hope that those pieces of seafood in the bisque weren't monkfish.

Because of its texture, monkfish can be grilled quite nicely without falling apart like some other types of fish. Here is one way of grilling monkfish.

grilled monkfish *serves 4*

2 lbs monkfish
½ cup olive oil
¼ cup lemon juice
1 tbsp Dijon mustard
chopped fresh dill

Cut the fish into 1-inch cubes. Mix oil, lemon juice, mustard and dill in a small bowl and pour over monkfish. Let fish marinate in the refrigerator overnight. Thread metal skewers with the fish and cook over a charcoal fire, turning until monkfish is tender, about 7 minutes per side. Serve over rice pilaf.

menu for day forty-seven

grilled monkfish
corn on the cob
tossed salad
rice pilaf
steamed vegetables

~~~ day forty-eight ~~~

Pretzels are one of my favorite treats. I have even gotten used to the unsalted variety. You can make your own pretzels and even though I have never done so myself, one of these days I will try my hand at it. Biscotti must be a distant cousin of the pretzel. I made some for the annual summer corn roast from time to time and just about everyone wants the recipe. It's a small effort but well worth it.

biscotti *serves 12*

5 cups flour	1 tbsp baking powder
¾ cup sugar	1 cup dry red wine
1 tsp salt	1 cup olive oil

Mix dry ingredients together, add wine and oil and mix, to form a soft dough. You will have to add more flour to keep dough from sticking. Divide dough in half and continue to divide the portions until you have 64 pieces. Roll each piece into a 3-inch crescent and place on greased cookie sheets, keeping them apart. Bake in a pre-heated 350° oven for 20 minutes and lower the heat to 300°. Continue baking until biscotti are golden brown, about 20 minutes. Cool on racks and serve. You won't have to worry about storing as there won't be any left over.

chicken teriyaki *serves 4*

½ cup olive oil
¼ cup lemon juice
2 tbsp soy sauce
fresh ground ginger
2 cloves garlic, minced
1 chicken, cut up

In a small bowl, mix oil, lemon juice, soy sauce, ginger and garlic. Pour over chicken and let marinate in the refrigerator overnight. Cook chicken over a medium hot charcoal fire, turning until chicken is done, about 25 minutes per side. Serve.

menu for day forty-eight

chicken teriyaki
tossed salad
bread and butter pickles
biscotti
cole slaw

~~~ day forty-nine ~~~

Many people marinate chuck steak but personally, I think it has too much fat and gristle. I personally use a leaner cut of meat and if it is not that tender, don't worry. The marinating process will make it so. Round roast or flank steak are fine. I made a beef marinade last year that wasn't bad except it had vinegar in it, which brought sauerbraten to mind. I love sauerbraten, but that wasn't what I had in mind when I made the marinade. The following marinade should not remind you of any German specialty.

marinated beef kebabs *serves 4*

¼ cup Dijon mustard
1 small onion, minced
fresh ground pepper
2 tbsp brown sugar
1 tsp Worcestershire sauce
¼ cup soy sauce
¼ cup bourbon
3 lbs sirloin tips

In a small bowl, thoroughly mix first seven ingredients. Pour over beef and marinate in the refrigerator overnight. Thread beef on metal skewers and cook over a hot charcoal fire until done to your taste. If you like, thread mushrooms, onion wedges, cherry tomatoes and green pepper pieces, or any combination, between the beef pieces before grilling. Serve.

I mentioned before that I had never made Buffalo chicken wings. I did make a batch of wings in the oven that came close to them. They may not be the real thing, but I think you will like them anyway.

Spanish chicken wings *serves 6*

2 tbsp ground cumin
2 tbsp Tabasco sauce
2 cloves garlic, minced
¼ tsp cayenne pepper
¼ cup red wine vinegar
1 tbsp paprika
3 tbsp olive oil
24 chicken wings

In a small bowl, mix cumin, Tabasco, garlic, cayenne, vinegar, paprika, and oil. Pour over the wings and marinate overnight in the refrigerator. Place wings on a wire rack over a cookie sheet and bake at 375° for 35 minutes, or until wings are tender. Serve.

pecan rice *serves 6*

2 tbsp olive oil
1 small onion, minced
2 cups long grain rice
½ tsp dried thyme
1 tsp summer savory
¼ tsp dried tarragon
3 cups chicken broth
¼ cup pecans, chopped
1 tsp Worcestershire sauce

Heat the oil in a heavy iron skillet on medium heat. Add onion and cook until onion is soft. Add rice, stirring to coat each grain. Add the remaining ingredients and bring to a boil. Lower the heat and simmer until broth is absorbed. Serve.

menu for day forty-nine

Spanish chicken wings
pecan rice
tossed salad
marinated beef kabobs
mashed rutabagas

You can find the recipe for the black beans and rice on page 170.

party number four

Chinese chicken wings
sweet and sour meatballs
Jell-O fruit mold
coq au vin
black beans and rice
Creole shrimp
macaroni tuna salad
Irish soda bread
roast round of beef
rice pilaf
vegetable tray with Russian dressing
sweet and sour red cabbage

I worked with Hank in the Boston area for a while and even had the chance to visit his lovely family in Maine. He had a large family and a large house and he was quite the cook, as was his wife Fran. Hank also had a great sense of humor and used to kid with his sons and daughters. One day one of the children asked what was on the menu for supper and he responded "Potatoes au gratin." One of the other kids then repeated, "We're having rotten potatoes?" To this, Hank only smiled and emphatically agreed.

~~~~~~~~~~~~~~~~~~~~~~
~~~~~~~~~~~~~~~~~~~~~~

8. Home again: just desserts

I returned to the town of my birth in May 1991. I had been in Western New York many times since moving away in 1968. My parents and my sister's family reside there as well as many friends, so it was not a difficult place to move to.

As far as desserts go, I love them but do not prepare too many of them myself and have them only occasionally. I have a few recipes of my own that I will share, but if you are looking for a great many finishing touches to meals, you will have to find them in another book.

Some of the best desserts that you will ever indulge in are loaded with butter, fresh whipped cream and of course, chocolate. I have seen many chocolate mousse recipes that use the yolks of the eggs as well as the whites. The recipe in this book uses only the whites, but the cream and chocolate more than make up for the decadence. I have gone one step further in a berry mousse recipe that uses strawberries instead of chocolate, but you'll have to live with the fat from the cream. Just remember that you are entitled to a treat every so often so don't despair.

This last suggestion for strawberry mousse brings up a very good idea: why not have fruit for dessert? Granted, each fruit has its season, but this way you can have dessert every day. Fresh pineapple is delicious, and if you have never tried kiwi fruit, you should give it a taste. You will be surprised at how good they are. Each spring I look forward to the arrival of the Bing cherries.

Unfortunately, their presence is short-lived. Don't forget mangoes, carambola, papaya, quince and some of the other unfamiliar foreign-looking fruit in the supermarket. If you do not try them, you'll never know if you'll like them.

My dad used to grow strawberries many years ago. Somewhere in the collection of home movies that my dad shot, is a frame of me with huge strawberries in my hand.

When the berries grow too close together, the result can be doubles, triples and even more than that. What you end up with is a huge strawberry that fans out and can weigh three ounces or more; and I held about three of those in my hand.

Homegrown strawberries are delicious. If you don't grow your own, you can certainly go out and gather your own. "Pick your own" farms can be found just about everywhere and they are not limited to strawberries. The benefits are freshness, a bit of exercise and cost savings. What you don't eat right away you can freeze. When I lived in Florida in 1988, I went out and picked four quarts of strawberries for one dollar. The following week I got eight quarts for the same price. I do believe that the strawberries grown in Florida are not as flavorful as those grown up north, but that's probably because of the soil differences.

I managed to do some strawberry picking in Western New York the spring after my return. It was well worth the effort. I picked enough to give some away to my family and friends. I should have charged them and made some money on the deal. What I couldn't eat I froze. Then some time after that I reached into the freezer and popped one of the frozen berries into my mouth. It was an excellent frozen delight, not unlike one of those frozen fruit bars but cheaper and good for you. I bet you can't eat just one.

Since I am on the topic of desserts, I recall what I said in the chapter on brunch with respect to the normalcy of breakfast foods. I worked with a guy who loved food as much as I do. He had an uncommon name, *Bernd*, but besides food, he appreciated a good beer as well. He mentioned that there were times when he would have a nice lobster dinner and then order his dessert. I don't think he was much into sweets, so what did he have for the clincher?

Another lobster.

~~~~~~~~~~~
~~~~~~~~~~~

~~~ day fifty ~~~

When I moved to my first house in Westchester, I invited one of my co-workers over for dinner. He brought his wife and son. Jeremy must have been no more than four years old. I had an ice cream freezer that I used only too rarely, so I decided to make lemon sherbet for dessert. Everyone had their sherbet and seemed to like it. As I was returning to the kitchen, young Jeremy intercepted me and asked if he could have more dessert. I guess he enjoyed it, or else that was the only food I made that he liked.

You can adapt the following recipe to lemon or orange, depending on your tastes.

lime sherbet *serves 6*

1 ½ cups sugar
2 cups water
14 oz lime juice
1 tsp grated lime rind
4 oz heavy cream, whipped

In a small saucepan over low heat dissolve the sugar in the water, stirring as necessary. Cool the syrup. Stir in the lime juice and the rind and refrigerate for 2 hours. Freeze the mixture in an ice cream freezer according to the manufacturer's directions until it is thick but not frozen. Blend in the whipped cream, transfer to a bowl, cover, and freeze until the sherbet is firm. Serve.

I never throw away stocks, sauces, or gravies. They can be used in a variety of recipes. I recall an occasion when I had some sauce left over from a chicken dish. I added it to a macaroni and ground beef casserole and the addition only improved the flavor. This may have been what prompted the following recipe.

Nepal spaghetti *serves 4*

2 cloves garlic, minced	28-oz tomato puree
1 large onion, chopped	3 tbsp curry powder
1 green pepper, chopped	½ tsp sugar
2 tbsp olive oil	1 lb thin spaghetti
1 lb ground turkey	

Sauté the garlic, onion, and green pepper in oil over moderate heat in a large Dutch oven. Add turkey and brown. Add puree, curry powder, and sugar and simmer for 45 minutes. Meanwhile cook spaghetti according to directions on the package. Drain spaghetti and serve the sauce over it.

You can buy curry powder or make your own. I prefer to make my own and just about any spice can be used. In addition to the spices in the recipe that follows, you could add chili powder, paprika, fennel seed, anise seed, ginger, and saffron, in any combination.

curry powder *makes about 3 tablespoons*

2 tsp ground cumin
2 tsp turmeric
¼ tsp cayenne pepper
½ tsp ground cloves
1 tsp fresh ground pepper
¼ tsp ground allspice
1 tsp ground cinnamon
¼ tsp ground nutmeg
2 tsp ground coriander

In a small bowl, mix all the spices thoroughly. Transfer to a small jar and store in a cool place.

menu for day fifty

Nepal spaghetti
tossed salad
lime sherbet
Cuban bread
cooked beets

~~~ day fifty-one ~~~

I have already mentioned my good friends Thom and Linda and their two sons. They paid me a visit in my first house and I prepared a dinner for them, which I can't remember, except for the dessert and soup. The latter was black bean soup, which is delicious but there are certainly more appealing looking soups. It is very dark in color, along the lines of grayish purple. At the time, their sons Karl and Ben were probably five and two years respectively.

While I was heating the soup, either Thom or his wife Linda, maybe both came over to see what was brewing. Upon glancing into the pot, a few derogatory comments followed. It was nothing personal, but let's face it: the soup looked wretched. Unfortunately, the ears of the children were not protected from the culinary abuse heaped upon me.

When we sat down to dinner, Thom and Linda both tried the black bean soup but Karl refused. Ben was just beginning to talk but the look on his face said it all. He would rather die than try the soup.

For dessert, I made chocolate mousse, which is also very dark in color. Apparently, the mousse is too similar in color to black bean soup because at least one of the boys refused it. Did you ever hear of anyone refusing chocolate mousse?

The story hardly ends here. It was during winter and there had been snow recently, so I had sprinkled some ashes from the fireplace on the outside sidewalk, the color being a purplish gray.

My guests thanked me for dinner and departed. On looking down at the sidewalk and the ashes sprinkled on top, Karl remarked, "Bob, did you put black bean soup on the sidewalk?"

So ends the black bean soup caper. Don't let this episode influence your decision to try mousse au chocolat or any dish with black beans.

black beans and rice *serves 6*

1 ¼ cups black beans	¼ tsp cayenne pepper
3 cups water	1 tsp sugar
¼ cup dry sherry	fresh ground pepper
2 large onions, chopped	1 green pepper, chopped
2 cloves garlic, minced	¼ tsp cloves
½ tsp oregano	boiled rice

2 large tomatoes, peeled and chopped

Place beans in a medium pan, cover with water, bring to a boil, cook for 2 minutes and let stand for 1 hour. Raise the heat and bring to a boil. Cook for 1 hour. Drain. Put beans back into the pan and add all remaining ingredients except the rice. Simmer for 1 hour or until beans are tender. Serve over boiled rice.

The chocolate mousse recipe that follows has been requested by just about everyone who has tasted it. The most amazing thing about this recipe is the simplicity.

mousse au chocolat *serves 8*

8 oz semi-sweet chocolate morsels
2 oz rum
3 tbsp sugar
4 egg whites
8 oz heavy cream

In a small saucepan over low heat, melt the chocolate morsels with rum, stirring to blend thoroughly. Whip egg whites with 1 tablespoon of sugar until they form peaks. Blend into the chocolate mixture. Whip the cream with remaining sugar and blend into chocolate mixture. Put mousse into a bowl, cover and refrigerate overnight. Serve.

A very popular appetizer is shrimp with spicy cocktail sauce. You can make your own cocktail sauce and you can make it as tangy as you want. It's simple and cheaper than buying the already prepared kind.

shrimp cocktail *serves 4*

1 cup ketchup
3 tbsp horseradish
1 tbsp lemon juice
1 tsp Worcestershire sauce
2 lbs cooked shrimp

Mix the ketchup, horseradish, lemon juice and Worcestershire sauce until thoroughly blended. Serve with the shrimp.

menu for day fifty-one

shrimp cocktail
tossed salad
black beans and rice
mousse au chocolat

~~~ day fifty-two ~~~

If you have ever been in Times Square in Manhattan, you probably have seen the small places selling Orange Julius. The drink is made with a few ingredients in a blender and is something one must try. You can also buy a pineapple Julius or strawberry Julius. I have made the drink myself and it is easy, delicious, and healthy. A dessert that you will enjoy is frozen Orange Julius.

frozen Orange Julius *serves 6*

juice of 6 oranges	1 tbsp vanilla extract
½ cup milk	4 tbsp sugar
1 cup water	1 cup crushed ice

Mix all the ingredients in a blender. If you use ice cubes, be sure to completely crush them. Transfer to a small container, cover and freeze overnight. Serve slightly thawed.

Coq au vin can be made in a Dutch oven on top of the stove or in a casserole dish in the oven. I have prepared it both ways. There are recipes for the entree with white wine but the recipe that follows uses dry red wine. Who said you can't have red wine with chicken?

coq au vin *serves 6*

1 chicken, cut up
5 tbsp flour
3 tbsp olive oil
1 large onion, chopped
1 slice ham, chopped
1 sprig parsley, minced
½ lb mushrooms, sliced
1 bay leaf
½ tsp dried thyme
¼ tsp dried tarragon
2 cloves garlic, minced
fresh ground pepper
2 oz brandy
12 oz dry red wine

Dredge chicken in flour. In a heavy iron skillet, brown chicken in oil and transfer to an ovenproof casserole. Put onion, ham, parsley, mushrooms, bay leaf, thyme, tarragon, garlic and pepper on top of the chicken. Heat the brandy, pour over chicken and ignite. When the flames die down, add wine. Place casserole in a heated 300° oven and cook until chicken is tender, about 1 ½ hours.

Nothing compares to fresh peas. The only problem is that if you pick them from the garden, they are so good that by the time you get inside your kitchen there won't be any left. A close second to fresh peas is frozen baby peas.

steamed peas *serves 6*

1 cup water
10 oz frozen baby peas
1 tbsp butter
fresh ground pepper

In a small saucepan bring water to a boil. Add peas and simmer until peas are heated, about 3 minutes. Drain. Add butter and pepper and serve.

menu for day fifty-two

coq au vin
escarole orange salad
steamed peas
rice pilaf
basil tomatoes
frozen Orange Julius

~~~ day fifty-three ~~~

One dessert that I remember from early childhood is Jell-O pie. It's quite easy to make and all you need to start are two piecrusts. You can use graham cracker crusts or regular piecrust. Both types can be bought at the supermarket or you can make your own. I have made them from scratch at times. You can use any flavor Jell-O you like.

Jell-O pie *serves 8*

1 package of Jell-O
1 cup of sugar
1 cup of water
1 can chilled evaporated milk
2 graham cracker crusts
whipped topping

In a small saucepan bring Jell-O, sugar and water to a boil, stirring until sugar and Jell-O are completely dissolved. Cool. In a large bowl whip evaporated milk until it forms peaks and fold in the Jell-O mixture. Pour into piecrusts and refrigerate. Top with whipped cream or topping, if desired.

graham cracker crust

¼ lb margarine
2 cups crushed graham crackers

Remove margarine from the refrigerator and let it soften at room temperature. Cream with a wooden spoon and add the graham crackers; mix in thoroughly. Put the mix into a pie plate and form the crust with a wooden spoon.

Shrimp has plenty of flavor of its own but adding some garlic makes it better. Add some tomato sauce and vermicelli and you have an easy, delectable entree.

garlic tomato shrimp *serves 4*

4 cloves garlic, minced
2 tbsp olive oil
28 oz tomato puree
pinch of sugar
1 tsp dried basil
½ tsp dried red pepper
2 cups of water
1 bay leaf
2 lbs cleaned shrimp

In a heavy iron skillet, sauté garlic in oil until golden brown. Add puree, sugar, basil and red pepper and simmer for 30 minutes. In a small saucepan, bring 2 cups of water to boil with the bay leaf and add shrimp. Cook until shrimp is pink, about 2 minutes. Drain shrimp and add to the sauce. Simmer for 1 minute. Serve over thin spaghetti.

menu for day fifty-three

garlic tomato shrimp
vermicelli
tossed salad
French-style beans
Jell-O pie

~~~ day fifty-four ~~~

Oranges are an excellent source of vitamin C, but they are quite versatile as well. This next recipe uses them with pork.

orange pork chops *serves 4*

1 orange
4 lean pork chops
1 tbsp butter
¼ tsp nutmeg
¼ tsp cinnamon
1 ½ cups beef broth
1 tbsp brown sugar
1 tbsp cornstarch
2 tbsp orange juice

Peel orange and slice it. In a heavy iron skillet, brown the chops in butter. Sprinkle each chop with nutmeg and cinnamon and place a slice of orange on each. Add broth and sugar and simmer for 35 minutes. Remove chops and orange slices to a small dish. Bring broth to a boil. Mix cornstarch with orange juice and add to the broth. Stir until sauce thickens. Transfer pork and orange slices back to the sauce and simmer until pork is tender, about 10 minutes. Serve over boiled rice.

apple crisp *serves 8*

6 apples, peeled and sliced
1 tbsp lemon juice
1 tsp cinnamon
¼ tsp ground cloves
4 tbsp butter
½ cup sugar
½ cup flour
¼ cup chopped walnuts
whipped cream

In an ovenproof casserole mix apple slices with lemon juice, cinnamon and cloves. In a small bowl mix butter, sugar and flour to form a crumb topping. Mix in walnuts and sprinkle over the apples. Bake in a 375° oven for 35 minutes or until apples are tender. Serve with whipped cream, if desired.

menu for day fifty-four

Chinese chicken wings
boiled rice
apple crisp
orange pork chops
steamed vegetables

~~~ day fifty-five ~~~

strawberry mousse *serves 8*

1 pint strawberries
¼ cup sugar
1 envelope unflavored gelatin
¼ cup cold water
4 egg whites
½ pint heavy cream

Wash and remove stems on the strawberries. Puree in a blender and reserve half of the puree. You may have to add a small amount of water to puree the berries depending on how juicy they are. Pour the other half into a small saucepan with sugar and heat to boiling. Sprinkle gelatin over cold water and let stand for 1 minute. Mix the hot puree with gelatin and cold puree. Whip egg whites until they form peaks. Blend into the puree. Whip cream and fold into the strawberry mixture. Transfer to a small bowl, cover and refrigerate for at least 4 hours. Serve.

Hungarian goulash *serves 6*

3 lbs lean stew beef
4 tbsp flour
3 tbsp olive oil
fresh ground pepper
6 oz tomato paste
2 tbsp paprika
8 oz beef stock

Dredge the beef cubes in flour. In a heavy iron skillet over moderate heat, brown the beef on all sides in oil. Transfer to an ovenproof casserole. Add pepper, paste, paprika and beef stock to the casserole and place in a 325° oven. Bake until beef is tender, about 2 hours. Serve over egg noodles.

menu for day fifty-five

Hungarian goulash
tossed salad
dilled carrots
egg noodles
Polish dill pickles
strawberry mousse

~~~ day fifty-six ~~~

I have already mentioned some of my childhood culinary delights. One dessert that I always looked forward to was glorified rice. When I was younger I really did not care for rice that much. Presently, I eat rice with meals just about every day. This dessert is quite easy to make and a nice addition to any dinner party.

glorified rice *serves 8*

1 cup crushed pineapple
1 ½ cups tiny marshmallows
1 cup cooked rice
½ cup chopped walnuts
2 tsp lemon juice
1 ripe banana, diced
8 oz heavy cream, whipped

In a small saucepan heat the pineapple. Remove from heat. Add marshmallows, rice, walnuts, lemon juice and banana and blend thoroughly. Cool. Fold in the whipped cream. Chill overnight. Serve.

pineapple chicken *serves 4*

1 chicken, cut up
4 tbsp flour
3 tbsp olive oil
1 cup pineapple tidbits
2 large onions, chopped
2 cups beef stock

Dredge chicken in flour. In a large Dutch oven over moderate heat, brown the chicken on all sides in the oil. Remove to a small dish. When the chicken is browned, put back into the pot and add pineapple, onions and beef stock. Cover and simmer until chicken is tender, about 45 minutes. Serve over boiled rice.

menu for day fifty-six

pineapple chicken
tossed salad
glorified rice
boiled rice
boiled brussels sprouts

party number five

mustard caraway wings
horseradish mushrooms
raisin rye bread
jambalaya
glorified rice
Indian green beans
mousse au chocolat
shrimp cocktail
lentil hummus
Hungarian goulash
egg noodles
picnic cole slaw
tossed salad

"Your food stamps will be stopped effective March 1992 because we received notice that you passed away. May God bless you. You may reapply if there is a change in your circumstances."
—Excerpted from a letter to a dead person from the Greenville County (South Carolina) Department of Social Services.

The above letter is authentic. I didn't make it up. I couldn't have.

~~~~~~~~~~~~~~~~~~~~~~
~~~~~~~~~~~~~~~~~~~~~~

9. Any leftovers?

This is the chapter that you won't find in ***The Read My Lips Cookbook***. Some people despise leftovers, but there are certain meals that you won't enjoy unless the entrée has a chance to season, such as some spaghetti sauces. My sauce on day two needs to be stored in the refrigerator overnight because the flavors haven't blended in to perfection on the day of creation – this is no reference to Genesis. On the other hand, the sauce with fresh tomatoes, garlic and basil on day thirty-seven can be served right after cooking it. It should be fine served the next day, as well, but the cold sauce on day thirty is most flavorful the same day. You could eat it next day, but it's best not to have any left over. This doesn't mean you can't eat it as midnight snack.

If *leftover* refers to any dish prepared the day before and you hate leftovers, it will be very difficult for anyone to cook for you. This chapter will feature some extravagant dinners, based on meals that I cooked for others over the last few years. These were posted on my web site over that same period and you can see that there's a bit more food – not necessarily more meat – than in the menus of the preceding chapters. In many cases, the food is prepared a day ahead, with the exception of the bread, which isn't quite as good as fresh out of the oven. By getting ready with some of the food the day before, you'll be able to sit down with your guests on the day of the dinner party. That's a good thing.

Many people at book signings ask about my web site, thinking I'm Bob Cook – they're half right about my name, and I do love to cook. The origin of the site name goes back to April 2002. On the way home from the writers' conference in Gettysburg, Pennsylvania, I decided to create a web site offering a few recipes from the cookbook – some of the better ones. I would start with six, and proceed to add another one every month. As time progressed, I begin posting recipes that weren't in the cookbook. As of late, the only time I put a recipe from the book would be if the time approached and I didn't have something new to add.

The result was a group of new offerings that those who bought the cookbook could add to their list of ideas to try. On occasion, the new recipe of the month turned out to be one that was already there, so eventually I deleted the lesser of the two. I also found that I could make a recipe better in some way, and this may have been the reason why I posted it there, even though an earlier version was already on the site. For example, tuna macaroni is better with fresh tuna – or thawed frozen. I came up with a real delight when I marinated the fish overnight, using the marinade in chapter 7. People loved this improvement on the original. I list it in this chapter along with a few other embellishments because invariably the change is done to make it tastier.

~~~~~~~~~~~
~~~~~~~~~~~

~~~ day fifty-seven ~~~

There are occasions when you can't cook a certain way because of what your guests won't or can't eat. Regardless, I don't find that much of a challenge, since you can improvise and still come up with an excellent dinner by omitting the offending ingredient, such as sugar, salt or wheat. I prepared the menu that follows on April 19, 2008 and did it without using wheat products, bananas, egg whites or whey. I didn't use curds either. I had an unexpected guest that day – he didn't break into my condo, but came with friends. I didn't mind his presence in the least and Rich raved about the soup, and continued doing so afterwards with his girlfriend, Sharon. It was later that I learned that Rich is a severe diabetic.

Besides these two, the others guests that day were my sister Pat and her husband, Lou, Sharon's sister Donna and her spouse, Randy. As you can see from the menu that follows, I didn't bake any bread that day, but I probably could have done so, using spelt flour, which everyone could have eaten. I have to do more research on spelt, and eventually I will make bread using it.

It must have been in early 2009 that I was told that ***The Read My Lips Cookbook*** was political. The person – I probably shouldn't use that word – came up with that conclusion without reading the book. At least that's what I think. This creature probably never even opened it. I expound on this strange tale a bit in ***Mirror, Mirror, On My***

Car, my 2009 book on truth. In an attempt to bring this individual's conclusion to being more truthful, I have to include this soup, which freezes quite well, provided there's any left. I recommend using Hungarian paprika. The name comes from the fact that the pinto beans and the paprika give it an orange hue. As you know, that color is a combination of red and yellow. One of the definitions of *yellow* is cowardly or *chicken.* You also know about the red states. Hence, the name, chicken Republican soup.

chicken Republican soup *serves a lot*

2 cups pinto beans
water
2 smoked pork chops, boned and cubed
2 cloves garlic, minced
1 bay leaf
½ lb smoked sausage, sliced
1 carrot, sliced
1 stalk celery, chopped
1 large onion, chopped
1 cup rutabaga, cubed
1 tbsp paprika
1 potato, finely grated
fresh ground pepper
2 Tbsp parsley

Cover beans with water, bring to boil, lower heat and cook for two minutes. Turn off heat and let stand for 1 hour. Add pork, garlic and bay leaf. Bring to boil, lower heat and simmer for 1 hour. Add sausage, carrot, celery, onion, and rutabaga and continue simmering for ½ hour. Add remaining ingredients and simmer for ½ hour more. Serve.

I hadn't made this dish for some time, but I modified the original recipe and used raspberry wine vinegar as well as fresh tarragon – a wonderful herb – which I grow in my well-lighted spare bedroom.

raspberry tarragon chicken *serves 6*

3 split chicken breasts plus 5 drumsticks

3 tbsp olive oil	1 tbsp tomato paste
3 cloves garlic, minced	1 cup white wine
1 onion, chopped	fresh tarragon
½ cup raspberry wine vinegar	1 tbsp parsley
fresh ground pepper	¼ cup chicken broth

Cut chicken breasts into pieces, brown them and drumsticks in the 2 tablespoon of oil in iron skillet. Remove to Dutch oven and sauté garlic in remaining oil in skillet for 5 minutes. Add onion and sauté. Add to remaining ingredients and pour over chicken. Bring to boil, lower heat and simmer for 40 minutes. If gravy is desired, dredge chicken in flour before browning or simply thicken liquid with 1 tbsp cornstarch after cooking. Serve.

I've mentioned the wonders of vinegar in a few of my books, especially the fact that it is a great environmental replacement for Drano. There is no reason in the world to use the latter: that chemical is not that effective and it's polluting. On the other hand, vinegar mixed with baking soda can not only clear up a slow drain, it can also unplug a stopped one. Besides that, it adds so much flavor to soups, dressings and main dishes. German potato salad would be dull without it, as would numerous other dishes.

What follows is a great appetizer that people rave about. For a going away party on June 24, 2005, I made it, along with Chinese chicken wings and marinated mushrooms. You can make it a day ahead, so it's really appropriate for the chapter, and it's quite easy.

citrus marinated shrimp *serves 8*

1 lime	3 tbsp catsup
3/4 cup water	1 tbsp sugar
1 bay leaf	1 tbsp Tabasco
1 lb peeled shrimp	½ tsp celery seeds
1 clove minced garlic	½ cup olive oil
1 tsp mustard seeds, crushed	1 onion, sliced thin

1 orange, peeled, quartered and sliced

Slice lime in half, juice it and reserve liquid. In medium sauce pan, bring water to boil, add bay leaf, lime halves and shrimp and cook for 2 minutes, or until shrimp are pink. Discard bay leaf and lime rind, drain shrimp and refresh with cold water. Mix lime juice and remaining ingredients and pour over shrimp. Mix, refrigerate and let marinate for 24 hours. Serve as appetizer or in buffet.

You can serve this delight at Thanksgiving dinner, but you need not wait until then to enjoy it.

cranberry Jell-O salad *serves 8*

½ cup cranberry juice
2 tbsp lemon juice
juice from can of crushed pineapple
1 package cherry gelatin
16 oz can whole cranberry sauce
8 oz can crushed pineapple, drained
½ cup fine chopped celery

In small saucepan, bring cranberry, lemon and pineapple juices to boil. Remove from heat and add gelatin, stirring until dissolved. Add cranberry sauce and stir, breaking up with fork. Refrigerate until gelatin is set, about 1 hour. Blend in pineapple and celery and pour into serving dish. Cover and chill until firm. Serve.

broccoli pasta salad *serves 6*

½ cup frozen sweet peas
2 cup broccoli flourettes
1 lb elbow macaroni
½ half cucumber, sliced
1 tbsp dried basil
2 tbsp prepared mustard
½ cup mayonnaisse
1 tbsp horseradish
fresh ground pepper
½ cup olive oil
½ teaspoon turmeric

Place peas in colander and run cold water over to thaw. Drain in colander. Cook broccoli for 5 minutes and drain. Cook pasta according to package directions. Drain. In large bowl, mix peas, macaroni, broccoli and remaining ingredients. Refrigerate for 2 hours. Serve.

menu for day fifty-seven

citrus marinated shrimp
cranberry Jell-O salad
chicken Republican soup
raspberry tarragon chicken
tossed salad with sesame ginger dressing
Chinese cabbage
glorified rice
mixed fruit
broccoli pasta salad

~~~ day fifty-eight ~~~

In the beginning of November 2008, I cooked dinner for my proofreaders and editor. If you are a writer, it's important to serve dinner for them and keep them happy. This is really important if you don't pay them, which I think you should do. If what you cook sends people to the emergency room, I'd advise taking them to a restaurant, unless you have a wealth of people to check your manuscripts. What follows is that meal, although Barb brought a really decadent dessert and I had pear sauce – similar to applesauce – and Kosher dill pickles from Charlie and Marge of Albion, a town about forty miles east of here.

A few years ago, friends of mine gave me a package for making soup, including herbs and beans. You had to add a few ingredients. The result was outstanding. Over time I figured out what spices to use as well as other ingredients that could produce an even better soup – one thing I try to do with recipes I make. Just recently I had a few things in my freezer – not road kill – that I thought I could add to the soup to help free up that portion of my freezer. Feel free to do likewise, but this advice is not intended for Jeffrey Dahmer.

For the beans, use 2 tablespoons each of split peas, lentils, pinto beans or whatever you have available. Feel free to use any vegetables available, as well as fresh herbs. On one occasion, I added Swiss chard and a lentil dish that I froze. Everything else in the mix will hide any dish you made that fell a bit short.

To thicken the soup, you can use cornstarch, flour, grated potato – or even mashed potatoes – rice, pasta or okra. You can make a huge pot and freeze for another occasion or use at a dinner buffet. The recipe that follows is roughly the way I made it for Christmas 2007.

French market soup *serves a lot*

2 tbsp each various dried beans

water	chopped fresh tarragon
2 boneless chicken breasts	1 tsp dried thyme
¼ lb smoked sausage	1 onion, chopped
2 cloves garlic, minced	2 cups sliced celery
1 large carrot, sliced	2 tbsp olive oil
1 tsp chicken bouillon	3 tbsp flour
½ tsp dried sage	1 potato, grated
½ tsp dried rosemary	fresh ground pepper

Place dried beans into large pot, cover with water and bring to boil. Cook for 2 minutes and let sit for 1 hour. Bring back to boil and cook for 30 minutes. To cooked beans add more water and chicken, sausage, garlic, carrot, bouillon and spices. Bring to boil, lower heat and simmer for 30 minutes. Remove chicken, let cool and chop. Sauté onion and celery in oil until soft. Add flour and continue stirring to make roux. Add chicken to pot with roux and simmer for 20 minutes. Add potato and simmer for 20 minutes more. Season with pepper and serve.

onion rolls *makes 16 rolls*

2 tbsp dry yeast
1 tsp sugar
1 cup lukewarm water
1 cup milk
2 tbsp brown sugar
2 tbsp olive oil
1 tsp salt
3 tbsp caraway seed
5 tbsp minced onion
1 cup rye flour
3 cups white flour

Proof yeast with sugar in water. Heat ½ cup milk, brown sugar and oil in medium saucepan until sugar is dissolved. Pour into large mixing bowl and add remaining milk. Cool and add yeast mixture. Add remaining ingredients and mix, adding as much additional white flour as needed and continue mixing until dough is stiff. Turn dough onto floured board and knead for 2 minutes or until dough is smooth and elastic. Wash out mixing bowl, dry out thoroughly and grease with olive oil. Put dough back into bowl, cover with damp towel and put into warm oven to rise until double in bulk, about 1 hour. Divide dough in half, half again and then divide each into four pieces. Roll each piece into ball, place 8 rolls each on 2 greased cookie sheets and flatten slightly. Place into oven and let rise again, about 45 minutes. Bake at 400° for 15-20 minutes until rolls are browned. Remove from oven and cool on medal rack. Serve.

I make the above rolls a bit different by doing the same thing I do when starting to create French onion soup. When the onions are golden brown or even darker, don't add the flour to make the roux, but place into a large bowl and cool. Proceed from there. These rolls take two and a half hours from start to finish.

Austrian cabbage *serves 8*

2 cloves garlic, minced	3 tbsp mustard
3 tbsp olive oil	½ cup white wine
1 large onion, chopped	2 tbsp caraway seed
14 oz can sauerkraut, drained	fresh ground pepper
3 cups cabbage, shredded	

In large pan, sauté garlic in oil over low heat for 7 minutes. Add onion and cook for 5 minutes. Add sauerkraut and cover, cooking for 10 minutes. While this is simmering, steam cabbage for 5 minutes. Add it and remaining ingredients to pan and simmer for 15 minutes more. Serve.

menu for day fifty-eight

Hungarian goulash	pear sauce
tossed salad	egg noodles
Austrian cabbage	onion rolls
Kosher dill pickles	coffee
French market soup	dessert by Barb

~~~ day fifty-nine ~~~

On the last Friday of October 2007, I cooked dinner for my cousin Maria, her son Michael and Maria's fiancé at the time, Drew. They are now man and wife. My cousin brought the dessert from the Trappist Monks, which Mike wasn't crazy about, but he did rave about the greens, asking for a second helping. The soup, pilaf and bread were different that day from what you will find below. Follow the recipe in this book for wilted endive but use kale instead, collards or mustard greens. For the appetizer, I used cucumber, celery, green pepper and raw carrots, and for a dip, you can use ginger sesame dressing or Romesco mayo, which follows. The main entrée can be found in this book, listed as chicken with mushrooms.

I found a raspberry dressing, which consists of raspberry vinegar and olive oil. It was all right but I figured I could make it better. In the summer of 2007, I tried another similar dressing with the actual fruit. It was an improvement, but I still wasn't satisfied. At the end of October of 2007, I put together what follows. You may be able to enhance the salad by pouring this dressing over a green salad with peaches, nectarines or even mango.

raspberry dressing

1 cup fresh picked raspberries or frozen, thawed
2 Tbsp raspberry vinegar 1 cup canola oil
Mix all ingredients in a blender until smooth. Serve over salad greens.

You can use this as a dip for vegetables or as a salad dressing.

Romesco mayo *makes 2 cups*

1 clove garlic, minced
2 tbsp olive oil
1 onion, chopped
1 red pepper, minced
½ green pepper, minced
1 large tomato, peeled and chopped
¼ cup orange juice
1 cup mayonnaise
fresh ground pepper
¼ cup toasted sliced almonds

Sauté garlic in oil until golden. Add onion, peppers and cook until soft, about 10 minutes. Add tomato, orange juice and simmer for 5 minutes. Remove from heat, add mayonnaise, ground pepper and almonds and puree in blender. Cover and refrigerate until time for use.

Oatmeal is a great way to reduce cholesterol. Add it to a bread recipe, and you can't go wrong.

oatmeal bread *makes 2 loaves*

1 ½ cups rolled oats
2 cups water hot water
2 cups water
1 tbsp dry yeast
1 tbsp olive oil
½ cup molasses
1 cup rye flour
5 cups of flour

In large bowl, pour hot water over oatmeal, stir and cool. This will take about an hour. Proof yeast in almost lukewarm water with sugar, and when oatmeal has cooled down, add yeast mixture, oil and molasses. Use ice cube or two, if necessary to aid cooling. Add rye flour and stir. Add white flour, stir and continuing adding enough flour until ingredients are blended. Place dough mixture onto floured board and kneed for five minutes, until dough is satiny. Wash bowl, dry, and grease with olive oil, adding dough. Cover with moist towel and let rise until double, about 1 hour. Place dough back onto floured board; work dough, dividing in half. Form into 2 loaves and place into greased bread pans and let rise for 40 minutes or until double. Bake at 400° for 1 hour. Remove loaves from pans and cool on a bread rack. Serve and enjoy.

When I make round loaves of bread, I use two bowls, one of ovenproof glass and the other of stainless steel. Since the dough rises but also spreads out on the cookie sheet, the result will be flatter loaves. This you can change with the bowls.

You may be wondering what to do with that leftover turkey. There are so many options, including this recipe. If you're not a big fan of curry, just omit it, since there's plenty of flavor without it. You can also make a few additions to the recipe such as tomatoes, peppers, smoked sausage and the appropriate seasoning and have a Cajun soup or turkey gumbo. You'll find recipes for curry seasoning and Cajun seasoning in this book, but you'll have to buy the gumbo file at the store.

turkey soup *serves 8*

turkey carcass
1 bay leaf
water
1 tsp thyme
fresh ground pepper
3 carrots, peeled and sliced
1 potato, washed and cubed
2 stalks celery, sliced
1 tbsp curry powder
1 tsp rosemary
½ cup cooked rice
1 large onion, minced

Place carcass into large pot with bay leaf and cover with water. Bring to boil, lower heat and simmer for 45 minutes. Remove carcass and let cool. Add remaining ingredients and simmer for 30 minutes or until vegetables are soft. Remove turkey from bones and add back to pot with any other cold turkey from bird. Simmer for 15 minutes more. Serve.

I was at an arts and crafts festival in the summer of 2009, when an individual asked if the recipes in ***The Read My Lips Cookbook*** had any preservatives in them. He mentioned food allergies and I didn't think too much about it and said, "definitely not." Sometime after I contemplated his question, wondering what cookbook would have any preservatives as ingredients. I certainly wouldn't want or recommend that book.

This cookbook has a few recipes that have been around for years, some with name brand labels, despite the preponderance of salt and other unhealthy additives, not to mention chemicals in those commercial products. This recipe I picked up by viewing a PBS program on vegetarian cooking, which I'm not that crazy about. You can find many recipes here and on my web site without meat – or perhaps only some chicken bouillon. This rice pasta pilaf gets much of its flavor from browning the vermicelli – or thin spaghetti, if you prefer – as well as the addition of the bouillon before adding the water. It might be familiar to you as *Rice-a-roni*, without all the sodium. I use no-sodium bouillon, but the regular kind is fine, too.

rice pasta pilaf *serves 6*

½ cup vermicelli, broken into ½ inch lengths
2 tbsp olive oil
½ cup basmati rice
1 tbsp low sodium chicken bouillon
2 cups water
¼ cup chopped fresh parsley or 2 tbsp dried

Brown vermicelli in oil over low heat in large skillet. Add rice and cook until it becomes almost clear. Add bouillon and cook for five minutes, stirring. Add water and parsley, bring to boil, lower heat and simmer until all water is absorbed. Serve.

menu for day fifty-nine

vegetables with dip
rice pasta pilaf
turkey soup
steamed vegetables
poulet sauté champignons
Oriental nectarine coleslaw
tossed salad with raspberry dressing
wilted kale
oatmeal bread
coffee
fruit cake

~~~ day sixty ~~~

Roughly speaking, this is the menu I created for a dinner at my home on March 24, 2007. As you can see, it's nearly vegetarian. I didn't make the shrimp that night, but I offer it here anyway. If I didn't bring out butter for the bread or milk for the coffee, it would have been vegan. I bought the pie from the supermarket and baked it in the morning of the event. To make the onions and peppers, follow the baloney and onions recipe for day 7 and *omit the baloney*. That sounds like what Congress should do while in session.

This pineapple rice pilaf will accompany seafood as well. You can use 3 strings of saffron or 1/4 teaspoon of the powder, or omit it if it's not in your kitchen.

pineapple rice *serves 8*

1 small onion, minced
2 tbsp olive oil
1 ½ cups rice
saffron
8 oz crushed pineapple
3 cups chicken broth
1 bay leaf

Sauté onion in oil in large skillet over medium heat until soft. Add rice and cook for 2 minutes. Add remaining ingredients and bring to boil. Lower heat and simmer until all broth is absorbed. Serve.

You don't need meat to create a delicious, healthy soup and you can make it a day ahead.

curried broccoli soup *serves 8*

1 ½ lb broccoli
2 cloves garlic, minced
2 tbsp olive oil
1 large onion, sliced
1 tbsp curry powder
6 cups chicken stock
¼ tsp thyme
¼ cup rice
1 bay leaf
¼ cup milk
croutons

Separate broccoli into flowerets and slice stalks. Select 8 small flowerets of broccoli, cook for 3 minutes, drain and set aside. Sauté garlic in oil in saucepan over medium heat for 2 minutes. Add onion, curry powder and cook until onions are soft. Place onions and garlic along with the stock, remaining broccoli, thyme, rice and bay leaf into Dutch oven or soup pot and bring to boil. Lower heat and simmer for 20 minutes or until rice is soft. Cool mixture and then blend in batches. Refrigerate overnight. On day of dinner, add milk and reheat. Place one reserved floweret in each bowl, pour soup over and add croutons. Enjoy!

orange baked beans *serves 8*

1 lb pinto beans
water
2 tbsp brown sugar
1 onion, chopped
8 oz tomato sauce
3 tbsp ketchup
1 apple, sliced
3 tbsp prepared mustard
½ cup hickory barbecue sauce
1 orange, peeled and cubed
½ green pepper, chopped

Soak beans overnight. Drain and rinse thoroughly. Place soaked beans into large Dutch oven and add water to just cover. Bring to boil, lower heat and cook for ½ hour. Pour off most of water and pour beans into crockpot. Add remaining ingredients and simmer over low heat for 12 hours. Serve.

menu for day sixty

Creole shrimp
curried broccoli soup
Russian brown bread
pineapple rice
tangy applesauce
onions and peppers
orange baked beans
Chinese cabbage
blueberry pie
coffee
tossed salad with sesame dressing

~~~ day sixty-one ~~~

On August 4, 2007, I had guests over for dinner and prepared the items that you see below – for the most part. I didn't make dessert, as Reg and Lynn brought it. The soup I made that day wasn't what you'll find listed below, as I came up with the Moroccan soup over a year after the day of this dinner.

This dinner may seem to be complicated, but it really won't take much elapsed time and is well worth the small effort. You can even warm any vegetable you prepare a day ahead as well as the egg noodles – which I put in a stainless steel bowl – on the day of the dinner. All this means is that while your guests are sitting in the living room, you won't have to be in the kitchen, but can join them.

pork paprika *serves 6*

6 loin pork chops
1 clove garlic, minced
1 tbsp caraway seeds
2 tbsp paprika
fresh ground pepper
1 cup white wine
8 oz tomato sauce
¼ sugar
½ cup water
1 tbsp cornstarch

Place chops in casserole dish and sprinkle garlic on top, followed by caraway, paprika and pepper. Pour wine on top and put casserole in refrigerator and let marinate for 3 hours. Remove dish and place pork onto platter. Stir tomato sauce and sugar into marinade mixture, put chops back into casserole dish and pour mixture over pork. Bake in preheated 300° oven for 1 hour, cool and put in refrigerator overnight. Next day, place dish into preheated 350° oven for ½ hour. Remove chops to meat platter and pour liquid into small saucepan and bring to boil. Mix cornstarch with water and add to wine / sauce mixture, stirring. Cook for 2 minutes. Replace pork in casserole and pour gravy over and bake for 20 minutes more. Remove and serve.

You can grow cilantro in your garden – I've grown it in my spare bedroom. It's an annual that acts like a perennial. Once planted, it grows to maturity and you can use both the leaves as well as the seeds in cooking. In addition, as the seeds fall to the ground, this will enable more plants to sprout the next year and in the years that follow. You shouldn't have to plant it again. This soup features that fine herb.

Moroccan soup ***serves 8***

1 cup lentils
1 large onion, chopped
1 cup chopped parsley
1 bunch cilantro, chopped
fresh ground ginger
½ tsp ground cinnamon
2 tbsp olive oil
15 oz can chopped tomatoes
2 cups chicken broth
15 oz can pea beans
2 tbsp flour
2 tbsp lime juice
1 tbsp tomato paste
½ cup thin spaghetti
fresh ground pepper

In small saucepan, cover lentils with water and cook for 2 minutes. In Dutch oven, sauté the onion, parsley, half the cilantro, ginger and cinnamon in oil over low heat for 5 minutes. Add tomatoes, broth, beans, lentils and 4 cups water and bring to boil. Lower heat and simmer for 45 minutes or until lentils are tender. In small bowl, whisk flour in 1 cup of water, stir in remaining cilantro, lime juice, tomato paste and add to soup with spaghetti and pepper. Simmer until pasta is soft, about 5 minutes. Serve.

menu for day sixty-one

mustard caraway wings
Moroccan soup
pork chops paprika
oatmeal bread
marinated vegetables
egg noodles
Austrian cabbage
peanut butter cake
coffee
tossed salad

~~~ day sixty-two ~~~

The Authors Guild of Western New York met at my home on Saturday, January 12, 2008. We had a discussion of future events as well as how to get out the word on our books and then settled down to dinner. I cooked a few things, and the menu for that event is included here. Of the people in the Guild at that time, four of the writers departed the group since that dinner – not all made it to the event. I'm happy to report that we have new blood as three writers have joined the Guild in 2009, and I'm continuing in the recruiting effort.

Oriental mayonnaise dip

cup of mayonnaise
2 tbsp soy sauce
1 tbsp sesame oil
fresh ground ginger

Combine all ingredients. Blend until thoroughly mixed. Serve with vegetables.

For this recipe, you can use any flavor pudding you desire.

pistachio tarts

1 package instant pistachio pudding
milk
1 cup whipped topping
individual serving graham pie shells

Prepare pudding as directed. Blend in whipped topping. Refrigerate for one hour. Pour into individual serving graham pie shells. Chill for 4 hours. Serve.

menu for day sixty-two

vegetable tray with Oriental mayonnaise dip
onion rolls
sausage lentil soup
garlic shrimp pasta
tossed salad with various dressings
Chinese cabbage
pistachio tarts

~~~ day sixty-three ~~~

I added the menu suggestion feature to my web site quite a while ago, but it was a long time since I changed it in the summer of 2009 from the old to this one, which is from Thursday, August 13, 2009. The beet recipe was suggested by a woman I met somewhere over the summer of that same year at some arts and crafts festival. My recipe may not be the way she fixes it, but it's close, easy and delicious. If you're not one who likes beets, you may change your mind after trying this recipe. Sorry that there's no dessert. You can come up with something. Pick something up at the supermarket or bakery.

Steelhead looks a bit like salmon, but it's really trout. Maybe they're cousins.

steelhead with almonds *serves 4*

4 steelhead trout filets
prepared mustard
¼ cup sliced almonds, toasted
¼ cup bread crumbs
Preheat oven to 350°. Place filets in small baking pan and spread mustard over trout. Sprinkle almonds on top, followed by bread crumbs. Bake for about 15 minutes. Remove and serve.

Cajun zucchini *serves 4*

2 tbsp of olive oil
1 medium zucchini, sliced
1 tbsp Creole seasoning
Warm olive oil in heavy skillet over medium heat, add zucchini, cover and cook for 5 minutes. Add Creole seasoning and cook for 5 minutes more, stirring. Serve.

If you've gotten this far, it means you've probably been avoiding fried foods. Many years ago, I made French fries from bacon grease and other types of animal fat that I collected. Then, they weren't called "freedom fries." The final product had great flavor, but wasn't very healthy. Besides those potatoes, I also did a batch of donuts and may have been a big threat to the success of Dunkin' Donuts. Yeah, right! You can still enjoy that potato delicacy but use canola oil. There's a better option than that. You can use curry seasoning, Creole seasoning, or any other spices to create this substitute to regular fries. I bake the cut up potatoes in the oven – they look just like fries and taste great, too. You might say that I have gained freedom from the grease and still have the security of comfort food.

baked French fries *serves 4*

4 large potatoes
1 tbsp paprika
2 tbsp olive oil
2 tbsp chili powder

Heat oven to 375°. Cut up potatoes into typical French fries, place in large oven dish or pan, and sprinkle with olive oil, paprika and chili powder. Stir to blend and place in oven. After 15 minutes, stir once more. Bake for another 15 minutes and remove and enjoy.

In my 2005 book, ***for seeing eye dogs only***, I mentioned that the government spent $100,000 to study why people don't like beets. I added my two cents by saying, "The people probably aren't cooking them." You should enjoy this recipe.

beets with bacon *serves 4*

4 large beets
3 tbsp vinegar
2 slices bacon
1 tbsp sugar

Wash beets and trim leaves and part of root. In large pan, cover beets with water and bring to boil. Lower heat and cook for 45 minutes. Meanwhile, fry bacon until crisp. Remove to paper towel and drain. Drain beets, cool, peel and mash, coarsely. Mix vinegar and sugar until sugar is dissolved. Blend in mashed beets along with the bacon and serve.

You may have figured that I wouldn't mention *Seinfeld* in this book, but think again. I experienced an episode in my kitchen that parallels the odor in Jerry's car. Thank goodness, it wasn't anything approaching what Jerry and Elaine had to sit through, but it was close.

Until recently, the best I could say about the vegetable, kohlrabi, was that I almost could spell it. In 2008, there were a few of these beauties in the bag of vegetables I received from Porter Farms. I heard it had the taste of a cabbage core – doesn't that sound delicious – and it appeared to me to be similar to potatoes in color and texture. I was told I had to peel it before cooking, but I decided I wanted the fiber from the peel. My choice was to make a soup in the crock pot with potatoes, kohlrabi, smoked Polish sausage and cabbage. I'm sure there were a few other ingredients, but they're not significant to the story. After simmering for hours – that really didn't help – I tried the recipe and wasn't that impressed. Not wanting to waste the stuff, I ate some of it and froze the rest, figuring I could blend a little here and there into other soup recipes.

That idea worked out well since there's none of it left and the other recipes weren't affected. However, on using my crock pot on a few occasions, I noticed a funny taste in a black bean recipe as well as in some other dish. Eventually I realized that the unpeeled kohlrabi forever deposited lasting taste into the porcelain of the crock pot. From now on, I'm peeling that sucker.

As far as I can guess, kohlrabi is probably a distant cousin of the radish family, maybe once removed for obvious reasons. Turnips could be relatives as well. In 2009, my vegetable bag had a few kohlrabi and I didn't cook them. Instead, I peeled them and pretended they were radishes. If you don't like radishes or turnips, you'll have to pass them off to someone else, pretend they're cabbage cores or cook them. As you might guess, they'll be no kohlrabi recipe here.

menu for day sixty-three

Cajun zucchini	beets with bacon
steelhead with almonds	corn on the cob
tossed salad	baked French fries

This is the menu I created for a party at my home on December 29, 2006 – more or less. People liked the sour dough bread I made, but I wasn't that enthusiastic, so it's not included here. Instead you'll find a recipe for zucchini bread, and a few other additions. For the party, if you make the jambalaya rather than the jambalaya pasta, you'll have potatoes, rice and pasta, although there's nothing wrong with two pasta dishes. The only items I had nothing to do with are the wine and dessert. Thanks go out to Julie for the cannolis; thanks to Mike for the Lambrusco and both for their help. Thanks to my sister Pat for the cookies.

In this cole slaw, peaches or nectarines can be used in place of the mango. Because of the strange pit, I find it challenging to remove the fruit around it.

almond cole slaw *serves 8*

1 mango
1 tbsp sugar
¼ cup white vinegar
½ cup toasted almonds
5 cups shredded cabbage
1 cup mayonnaise
1 onion, thinly sliced

Peel mango and dice. Dissolve sugar in vinegar in small bowl. Add to mango and remaining ingredients, stir to blend and chill. Serve.

My first experience with tabbouleh came in the 1970s. For those unfamiliar with that offering, it's made with cracked wheat, olive oil, lemon juice, chopped tomatoes and mint. As you may imagine, the dish is quite healthy, but it took me longer than I wanted to finish it. The following recipe should entice more people into partaking in a healthy Middle Eastern item.

•

citrus bulghur salad *serves 8*

16 oz cracked wheat
5 tbsp lime juice
3 tbsp orange juice
1 tbsp Dijon mustard
1 cup olive oil
½ tsp ground cumin
1 tsp cinnamon
1 cup sliced cashews
1 tbsp sugar
3 tbsp parsley
2 oranges, peeled and chopped
1 small onion, minced

Soak the cracked wheat for 1 hour in enough water to cover it by 1 inch. Squeeze water from cracked wheat by handful and place into large bowl. Mix juices, mustard and olive oil until blended. Add remaining ingredients along with dressing to cracked wheat and stir. Serve.

This is a slight variation on the bean with bacon soup for day 10. I have frozen it and used for another dinner.

onion bean soup *serves 8*

1 ½ cups pea beans	3 large onions, chopped
2 quarts of water	½ tsp sugar
½ tsp rosemary	3 tbsp flour
¼ tsp dried sage	1 large potato, grated
½ tsp dried thyme	1 tsp Tabasco sauce
2 tbsp olive oil	fresh ground pepper
2 garlic cloves, minced	3 tbsp vinegar

Soak beans overnight or cook beans with sufficient water for 2 minutes in Dutch oven and let stand for 1 hour. Drain, add 2 quarts of water and bring to boil and cook for 1 hour. Crush rosemary, sage and thyme in mortar and pestle. Add oil to frying pan and sauté garlic, onions, sugar and spices over medium heat until onions are brown. Be careful not to burn, but the darker they are, the better the flavor will be. Sugar helps to brown them. Add flour to pan, stirring for 2 minutes to make roux. Add onion mix to beans along with potato and bring to boil, lower heat and simmer for 1 hour. Turn off heat, add Tabasco sauce, ground pepper and vinegar. Stir well. Serve with baked croutons.

Some people put corn in their salsa, but I prefer not to, even though I love fresh corn on the cob in the summer. I had a delicious black bean salsa at a political gathering before the election in 2006. I wish I had gotten the recipe. This will have to suffice.

black bean salsa

½ cup chopped cilantro
1 small onion, finely chopped
15 oz can diced tomatoes
1 15 oz can black beans, rinsed and drained
4 oz can chopped green chilies
1 tsp ground cumin
In large bowl, mix all ingredients. Cover and refrigerate. Serve with tortilla chips.

I related the black bean caper on day 51 along with the mousse connection, but I experienced another event a few years later that's related. In early 2005, I was on channel 17, a PBS station in Buffalo for the program ***WNED COOKS: Q is for Quick and Easy***. I had seven minutes to make the chocolate mousse from this cookbook. I mentioned *quick* in the title of the program, but on preparing a batch the day before at home, it took me about fifteen minutes. Fortunately, Eileen Koteras was on the set, so I put her to work and we managed in the allotted time. The mousse was a huge hit as the people who tasted it raved and thought they were in heaven. People in Buffalo believe in an afterlife, with or without chocolate. Those in the studio were actually fighting over the dessert. Pasta dishes are good, and so are mushrooms stuffed with crab, all of which could be seen being produced in the studio for the show. However, that day ***mousse*** was king!

As far as healthy dishes go, this recipe is at the top. If people at your party don't like lentils, tell them it's a marinated bean dish.

marinated lentils *serves 8*

½ lb lentils, picked over ½ cup olive oil
2 large onions, finely chopped
½ cup sugar 2 tbsp dry mustard
3/4 cup red wine vinegar 3 tbsp parsley leaves
fresh ground pepper ½ cup white wine
½ tsp Tabasco sauce 1 tsp garlic powder
½ tsp Worcestershire sauce
3 tbsp fresh oregano or 1 tsp dried
Cook lentils in enough water to cover for 30 minutes. Drain. Add remaining ingredients, stir well and refrigerate overnight. Serve.

I try quite a few new recipes and as you probably know, even good cooks have their moments, and I'm not talking about those of senior citizens. Towards the end of September 2007, I had another huge zucchini from Porter Farms so I decided to try a new recipe for bread using that vegetable. After being in the oven for an hour or so, the bread looked fine, but I figured it would need a few extra minutes. When I checked it in the oven a short time thereafter, the top looked fine but the bottom resembled some kind of inedible soup. I wound up tossing it since another half-hour wouldn't have made a difference. Two more hours may have made it a bit too crunchy. The reason for the disaster was that I left out two cups of flour, which is exactly what the recipe called for.

You're probably wondering what to do with all that zucchini that you have, even though you don't have a garden. You have a few options, including the old standby, zucchini bread. Here's a recipe for it.

zucchini bread *makes 2 loaves*

3 eggs
1 ½ cups sugar
1 ½ cups olive oil
1 tbsp vanilla extract
1 zucchini, chopped
2 cups flour
2 tsp ground cinnamon
1 tsp ground allspice
½ tsp salt
1 tsp baking powder
1 tsp grated orange rind
1 tsp baking soda
¾ cup chopped walnuts
butter

Preheat oven to 325°. Place first 5 ingredients in blender and puree. Add to next 7 ingredients and blend thoroughly. Stir in walnuts and pour into 2 buttered bread pans. Bake for 1 hour 20 minutes or until done. Toothpick inserted into loaves should come out clean. Let loaves stand for 15 minutes. Turn bread onto rack and cool. Serve.

The tuna macaroni salad recipe for day 12 can be made so much better by marinating the tuna and grilling it. What follows is what I promised you at the beginning of this chapter.

grilled tuna pasta salad *serves 8*

2 medium tuna steaks
½ cup olive oil
6 tbsp soy sauce
½ cup sherry
2 tbsp snipped dill
fresh grated ginger
grated orange peel
1 lb elbow macaroni
1 cucumber, chopped
1 onion, chopped
fresh ground pepper
½ cup mayonnaise

Place tuna into medium bowl. In small bowl mix olive oil, 4 tbsp of soy sauce, sherry, snipped dill, ginger and orange peel and pour over tuna. Let marinate overnight. Next day, cook macaroni according to package directions. Drain and cool. Grill tuna over medium fire for 5 minutes per side, or until cooked through. Cool tuna and flake. Place macaroni into large bowl, add tuna, remaining soy sauce, cucumber, onion, ground pepper and mayonnaise. Mix and, if necessary, add more mayo. Refrigerate. Serve with basil tomatoes.

I found a recipe in my black book – I don't use mine for what others might – and I thought I'd make a few substitutions in order to use some zucchini. My editor must have liked it because he asked for seconds. If you're not a big fan of zucchini, don't worry – you won't even taste it.

zucchini casserole *serves 4*

1 zucchini, diced
1 onion, sliced
½ cup bamboo shoots
½ cup water
½ cup mayonnaise
fresh ground pepper
1 package long grain and wild rice
1 can cream of chicken soup
1 red pepper, thinly sliced
1 cup French style green beans

In large bowl, mix all ingredients, pour into large casserole dish, and bake for 35 minutes at 375°. Serve.

This recipe won an award in a cook-off in Buffalo on Super Bowl Sunday, a few years ago. Don't be put off by the number of ingredients. It's not that complicated, and well worth it. You can buy gumbo file at most large supermarkets. This recipe is finally going to be in this cookbook and perhaps it is a fitting last recipe. I certainly couldn't leave it out of the final party, since I made it for so many corn roasts over the years.

seafood gumbo *makes a lot*

3 tbsp olive oil
2 cloves garlic, minced
1 green pepper, chopped
2 cups of celery, chopped
1 large onion, chopped
3 tbsp flour
1 bay leaf
28 oz crushed tomatoes
3 whole cloves
½ tsp ground allspice
2 tbsp Creole seasoning
10 oz of chopped okra
12 oz seafood flakes
2 cups of water
½ cup cooked rice
1 tsp Tabasco sauce
1 tsp Worcestershire sauce
fresh ground pepper
1 ½ tsp gumbo file

Place olive oil in large frying pan over low heat. Sauté garlic for 2 minutes. Add green pepper, celery and onion and cook for five minutes. Add flour and continue stirring to make roux. Empty frying pan into stockpot and add bay leaf, tomatoes, cloves, allspice, Creole seasoning, okra, seafood flakes, and water. Bring to boil over moderately low heat. Lower heat and simmer for ½ hour. Add rice, Tabasco sauce, Worcestershire sauce, pepper and simmer for 1 minute more. Remove pot from heat and stir in gumbo file. Serve.

party number six

zucchini bread	German potato salad
onion bean soup	jambalaya pasta
marinated lentils	Lambrusco
seafood gumbo	cannolis
almond cole slaw	assorted cookies
black bean salsa and chips	zucchini casserole
grilled tuna pasta salad	citrus bulghur salad

vegetable tray with Romesco mayo
tossed salad with sesame dressing

I've enjoyed camping over the years at various locations in Massachusetts, Tennessee, Connecticut, Maine, Pennsylvania, Virginia, Florida, and the Maritime Provinces of Canada. We've had meals that were prepared before the trip – yeah, leftovers – on many occasions as well as food we prepared from scratch while on vacation. Naturally, we used the Coleman stove to prepare breakfast, including delicious home-brewed coffee. Once, one of the guys fixed pancakes, but on sitting down to eat and digging in, we discovered they needed a bit longer on the grill, so one of the campers commented, "Wow, cream filled pancakes."

~~~~~~~~~~~~~~~~~~~~~~
~~~~~~~~~~~~~~~~~~~~~~

recipe index

almond cole slaw 214

appetizers

- black bean salsa 217
- Chinese chicken wings 126
- citrus marinated shrimp 188
- Creole shrimp 136
- dilled shrimp 127
- horseradish mushrooms 124
- lentil hummus 154
- marinated lentils 218
- meatballs 10
- mustard caraway wings 140
- Oriental mayonaisse dip 207
- picadillo 128
- Romesco mayo 19
- shrimp cocktail 171
- Spanish chicken wings 160
- stuffed mushrooms 103
- sweet and sour meatballs 134

apple

- apple crisp 178
- spicy applesauce 67

apple crisp 178
Atlantic chop suey 89
Austrian cabbage 194
baked acorn squash 83
baked chicken 14
baked croutons 6
baked fish 43
baked French fries 211
baked potatoes 4

baloney and onions 19
barbeque sauce 72
barbequed chicken 71
basil tomatoes 36
bean with bacon soup 31
beans, dried
- bean with bacon soup 31
- black bean salsa 217
- black beans and rice 170
- Cajun beans and rice 40
- chicken Republican soup 186
- chili con carne 13
- French market soup 192
- green split pea soup 58
- hickory baked beans 26
- lentil hummus 154
- lentil sausage soup 152
- marinated lentils 218
- Moroccan soup 206
- orange baked beans 203
- three bean salad 113
- turkey minestrone soup 33
- yellow split pea soup 35

beef
- baloney and onions 19
- beef and onions 108
- beef stew 16
- beer and beef stew 28
- chili con carne 13
- grilled steak 3
- Hungarian goulash 180
- marinated beef kabobs 159
- meatballs 10

pan-fried steak 4
roast round 80
spaghetti with meat sauce 9
stewed hamburgers 34
sweet and sour meatballs 134
beef and onions 108
beef stew 16
beer and beef stew 28
beets and bacon 211
biscotti 157
black bean salsa 217
black beans and rice 170
boiled brussels sprouts 123
boiled cabbage 146
boiled rice 40
bread and butter pickles 111
breads
biscotti 157
cinnamon raisin bread 68
cinnamon walnut waffles 138
Cuban bread 55
dill rye bread 60
Irish soda bread 57
oatmeal bread 197
onion rolls 193
onion rye bread 63
raisin rye bread 73
Russian brown bread 51
zucchini bread 219
broccoli pasta salad 190
broiled smelts 114
bulghur pilaf 93

cabbage
almond cole slaw 214
Austrian cabbage 194
boiled 146
Chinese 70
cole slaw 106
lazy golabki 94
Oriental nectarine slaw 129
picnic cole slaw 137
sweet and sour red 90
vegetable Jell-O mold 92
Cajun beans and rice 40
Cajun zucchini 210
chicken
baked 14
barbequed 71
broth 44
cacciatore 56
Chinese wings 126
coating mix 30
coq au vin 173
curry 33
French market soup 192
Hong Kong 102
jambalaya 53
mustard caraway wings 140
Oriental stew 82
pineapple 181
raspberry tarragon chicken 187
rum 122
Spanish wings 160
tangy barbequed 148
tasty baked 30

teriyaki 158
with mushrooms 112
chicken broth 44
chicken cacciatore 56
chicken coating mix 30
chicken curry 133
chicken Republican soup 186
chicken shadow soup 39
chicken teriyaki 158
chicken wings
Chinese 126
mustard caraway 140
Spanish 160
chicken with mushrooms 112
chili con carne 13
Chinese cabbage 70
Chinese cauliflower 37
Chinese chicken wings 126
cinnamon raisin bread 68
cinnamon walnut waffles 138
citrus bulghur salad 215
citrus marinated shrimp 188
city chicken 91
cole slaw 106
cooked beets 11
coq au vin 173
corn on the cob 106
cranberry Jell-O salad 189
creamy mustard dressing 109
Creole seasoning 136
Creole shrimp 136
croutons 6
Cuban bread 55

curried broccoli soup 202
curry powder 168
desserts
apple crisp 178
frozen Orange Julius 172
glorified rice 181
Jell-O pie 175
lime sherbet 166
mousse au chocolat 171
pistachio tarts 207
strawberry mousse 179
dill rye bread 60
dilled carrots 18
dilled shrimp 127
egg noodles 17
escarole orange salad 58
fish chowder 25
French dressing 150
French market soup 192
French onion soup 130
French-style beans 5
frozen Orange Julius 172
fruit
apple crisp 178
escarole orange salad 58
Jell-O fruit mold 151
Oriental nectarine slaw 129
spicy applesauce 67
strawberry mousse 179
garlic cauliflower 81
garlic tomato shrimp 176
gazpacho 27
German potato salad 115

glorified rice 181
graham cracker crust 175
green beans
French-style 5
Indian 146
steamed 108
three bean salad 113
green split pea soup 58
grilled monkfish 156
grilled steak 3
grilled tuna pasta salad 220
hickory baked beans 26
Hong Kong chicken 102
horseradish broccoli 54
horseradish mushrooms 124
Hungarian goulash 180
Indian green beans 146
Irish soda bread 57
jambalaya 53
Jell-O
cranberry Jell-O salad 189
fruit mold 151
pie 175
vegetable mold 92
Jell-O fruit mold 151
Jell-O pie 175
lazy golabki 94
lazy pierogi 135
lentil hummus 154
lentil sausage soup 152
lentils
lentil hummus 154
lentil sausage soup 152

marinated lentils 218
lime sherbet 166
marinated beef kabobs 159
marinated lentils 218
marinated pork 155
marinated swordfish 145
mashed rutabagas 59
meatballs 10
meatless spaghetti 125
Moroccan soup 206
mousse au chocolat 171
mushrooms
chicken with mushrooms 112
horseradish mushrooms 124
stuffed mushrooms 103
mustard caraway wings 140
Nepal spaghetti 167
oatmeal bread 197
oil and vinegar dressing 6
onion bean soup 216
onion rolls 193
onion rye bread 63
orange baked beans 203
orange pork chops 177
Oriental chicken stew 82
Oriental mayonaisse dip 207
Oriental nectarine slaw 129
pan-fried steak 4
pasta, beans and rice
Atlantic chop suey 89
bean with bacon soup 31
black bean salsa 217
black beans and rice 170

boiled rice 40
broccoli pasta salad 190
bulghur pilaf 93
Cajun beans and rice 40
chicken cacciatore 56
chicken Republican soup 186
citrus bulghur salad 215
egg noodles 17
French market soup 192
glorified rice 181
green split pea soup 58
grilled tuna pasta salad 220
hickory baked beans 26
jambalaya 53
lazy golabki 94
lazy pierogi 135
lentil hummus 154
lentil sausage soup 152
marinated lentils 218
meatless spaghetti 125
Nepal spaghetti 167
orange baked beans 203
pecan rice 160
pineapple rice 201
rice pasta pilaf 200
rice pilaf 15
spaghetti with meat sauce 9
Spanish rice 88
summer spaghetti 105
three bean salad 113
tuna macaroni salad 36
Viennese rice 110
pecan rice 160

picadillo 128
pickles
bread and butter pickles 111
Polish dill pickles 107
picnic cole slaw 137
pineapple chicken 181
pineapple rice 201
pistachio tarts 207
poached cod 61
poached haddock 85
Polish dill pickles 107
pork
chicken Republican soup 186
city chicken 91
gravy 69
jambalaya 53
lentil sausage soup 152
marinated 155
orange chops 177
paprika 205
roast loin 66
spaghetti with meat sauce 9
with prunes 139
pork gravy 69
pork paprika 205
pork with prunes 139
potato salad 20
potato sprout soup 44
potatoes
baked 4
baked French fries 211
German salad 115
Russian salad 131

salad 20
sprout soup 44
raisin rye bread 73
raspberry dressing 196
raspberry tarragon chicken 187
rice
boiled 40
glorified rice 181
jambalaya 53
lazy golabki 94
pasta pilaf 200
pecan 160
pilaf 15
pineapple 201
Spanish 88
Viennese 110
with black beans 170
with Cajun beans 40
rice pasta pilaf 200
rice pilaf 15
roast loin of pork 66
roast round of beef 80
Romesco mayo 196
rum chicken 122
Russian brown bread 51
Russian dressing 86
Russian potato salad 131
salad dressings
creamy mustard dressing 109
French dressing 150
oil and vinegar dressing 6
Oriental mayonaisse dip 207
raspberry dressing 196

Romesco mayo 196
Russian dressing 86
sesame dressing 123
salads
broccoli pasta salad 190
citrus bulghur salad 215
cranberry Jell-O salad 189
escarole orange 58
gazpacho 27
German potato 115
grilled tuna pasta salad 220
Jell-O fruit mold 151
potato 20
Russian potato 131
three bean 113
tossed 5
tuna macaroni 36
vegetable Jell-O mold 92
sausage
baloney and onions 19
Cajun beans and rice 40
French market soup 192
green split pea soup 58
jambalaya 53
lentil soup 152
potato sprout soup 44
spaghetti with meat sauce 9
Viennese rice 110
seafood
baked fish 43
broiled smelts 114
citrus marinated shrimp 188
Creole shrimp 136

dilled shrimp 127
fish chowder 25
garlic tomato shrimp 176
grilled monkfish 156
grilled tuna pasta salad 220
marinated swordfish 145
poached cod 61
poached haddock 85
seafood gumbo 222
shrimp cocktail 171
shrimp scampi 62
steelhead with almonds 209
tuna macaroni salad 36
seafood gumbo 222
sesame dressing 123
shrimp
citrus marinated shrimp 188
cocktail 171
Creole 136
dilled 127
garlic tomato 176
scampi 62
shrimp cocktail 171
shrimp scampi 62
soups
bean with bacon 31
chicken broth 44
chicken Republican 186
chicken shadow 39
curried broccoli 202
fish chowder 25
French market 192
French onion 130

gazpacho 27
green split pea 58
lentil sausage 152
Moroccan 206
onion bean 216
potato sprout 44
seafood gumbo 222
turkey 198
turkey minestrone 33
yellow split pea 35

spaghetti
meatless 125
Nepal 167
spaghetti with meat sauce 9
summer 105
spaghetti with meat sauce 9
Spanish chicken wings 160
Spanish rice 88
spicy applesauce 67
steamed asparagus 154
steamed green beans 108
steamed peas 174
steamed vegetables 15
steelhead with almonds 209
stewed hamburgers 34
strawberry mousse 179
stuffed mushrooms 103
summer spaghetti 105
sweet and sour meatballs 134
sweet and sour red cabbage 90
tangy barbeque sauce 149
tangy barbequed chicken 148

tasty baked chicken 30
three bean salad 113
tossed salad 5
tuna macaroni salad 36
turkey
Atlantic chop suey 89
lazy golabki 94
minestrone soup 33
Nepal spaghetti 167
Oriental nectarine slaw 129
picadillo 128
soup 198
turkey minestrone soup 33
turkey soup 198
vegetable Jell-O mold 92
vegetables
almond cole slaw 214
Austrian cabbage 194
baked acorn squash 83
baked French fries 211
baked potatoes 4
basil tomatoes 36
beets and bacon 211
black bean salsa 215
boiled brussels sprouts 123
boiled cabbage 146
bread and butter pickles 111
broccoli pasta salad 190
Cajun zucchini 210
Chinese cabbage 70
Chinese cauliflower 37
cole slaw 106
cooked beets 11

corn on the cob 106
dilled carrots 18
escarole orange salad 58
French-style beans 5
garlic cauliflower 81
gazpacho 27
German potato salad 115
horseradish broccoli 54
Indian green beans 146
Jell-O mold 92
mashed rutabagas 59
Oriental nectarine slaw 129
picnic cole slaw 137
Polish dill pickles 107
potato salad 20
Russian potato salad 131
steamed 15
steamed asparagus 154
steamed green beans 108
steamed peas 174
sweet and sour red cabbage 90
three bean salad 113
tossed salad 5
vegetable Jell-O mold 92
wilted endive 17
zucchini casserole 221
vegetable Jell-O mold 92
Viennese rice 110
wilted endive 17
yellow split pea soup 35
zucchini bread 219
zucchini casserole 221

Breinigsville, PA USA
25 April 2010
236734BV00001B/2/P

9 780981 784366